EARLY JAZZ GREATS

PAPA CHARLIE JACKSON

RAMBLIN' THOMAS

LEROY CARR and SCRAPPER BLACKWELL

EARLY JA

MEMPHIS MINNIE

BIX "BEIDERBECKE

HARRY "MAC" McCLINTOCK

JOE "WINGY" MANNONE

EARLY JAZZ GREATS

TED GO
TED GOSSETT

BLIND WILLIE JOHNSON

SIDNEY BECHET

EARLY JAZZ GREATS

CHARLEY PATTON

JIMMY BLYTHE

EARLY JAZZ GREATS

ED

"JELLY ROLL" MORTON

EARLY JAZZ GREATS

"DOCK" BOGGS

LIL HARDIN

EARLY JAZZ GREATS

ANDY PALMER of JIMMIE JOHNSON'S STRING BAND

JIMMY NOONE

EARLY JAZ

STEVE BROWN

# HEROES OF
# BLUES, JAZZ
# & COUNTRY

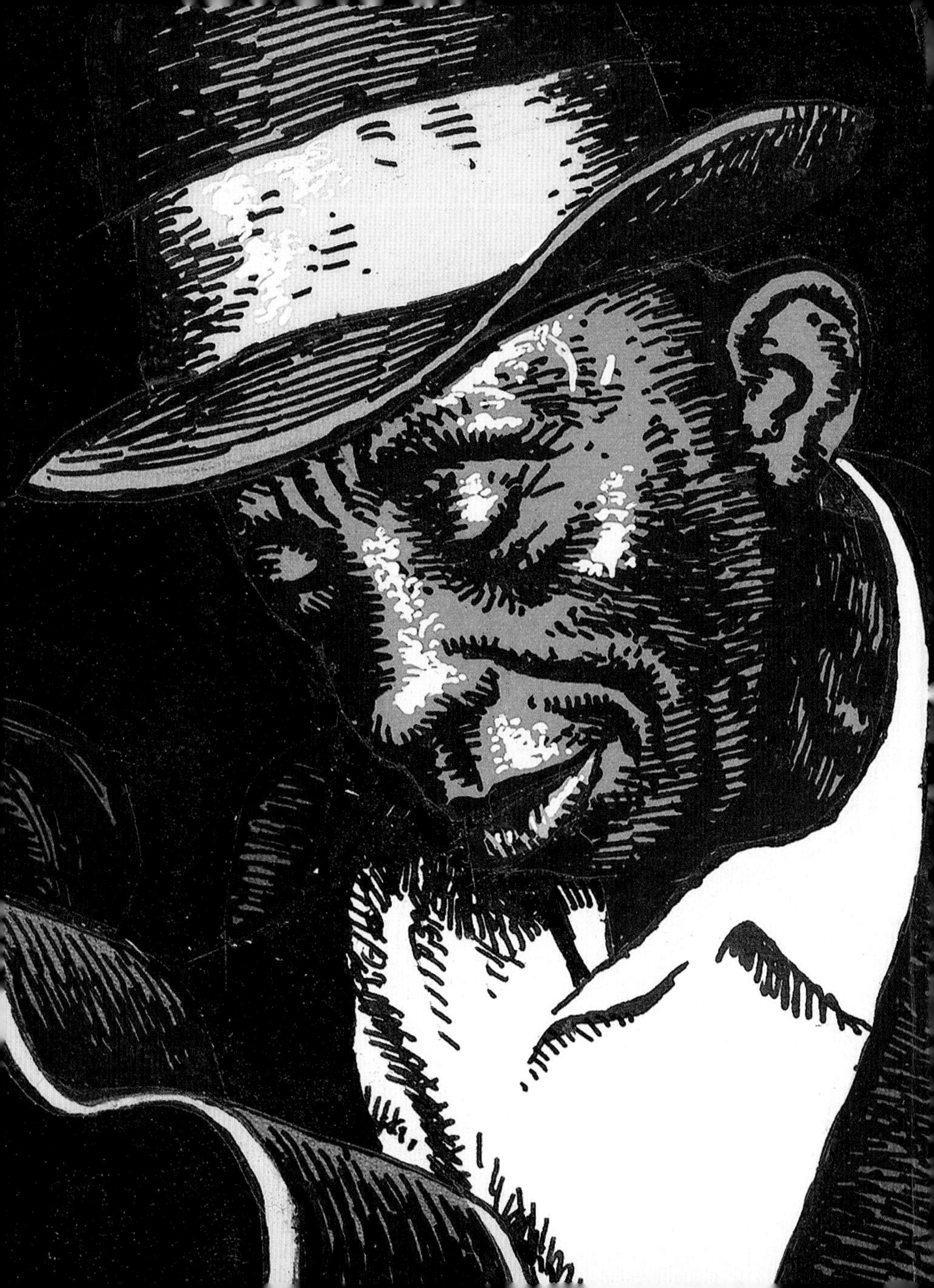

# R. Crumb's
## HEROES OF
# BLUES, JAZZ
# & COUNTRY

ILLUSTRATED BY
**R. CRUMB**

TEXT BY
**STEPHEN CALT,
DAVID JASEN,** AND
**RICHARD NEVINS**

INTRODUCTION BY
**TERRY ZWIGOFF**

ABRAMS, NEW YORK

# CONTENTS

## HEROES OF THE BLUES

# EARLY JAZZ GREATS

# PIONEERS OF COUNTRY MUSIC

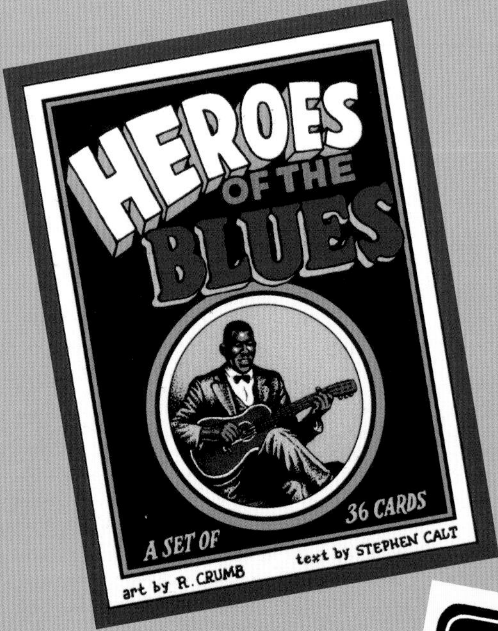
HEROES
OF THE
BLUES
A SET OF
36 CARDS
art by R. CRUMB
text by STEPHEN CALT

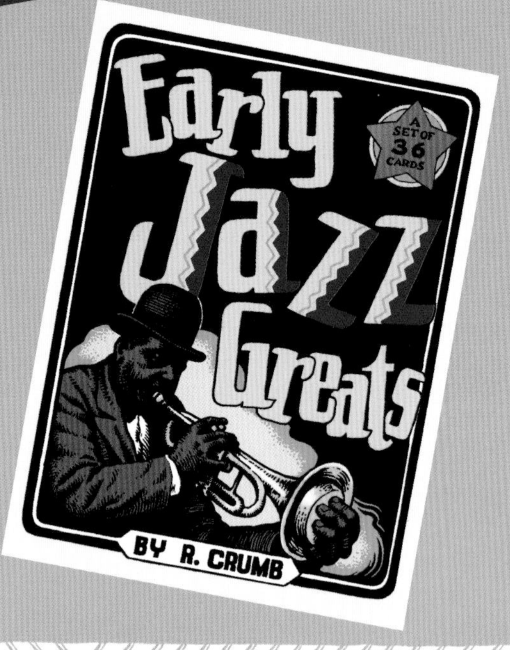
Early
Jazz
Greats
A SET OF 36 CARDS
BY R. CRUMB

# INTRODUCTION

## Terry Zwigoff

I met Robert Crumb in 1970 and we quickly became friends, sharing a love for 1920s and '30s music and trying to figure out how to play this music ourselves. One of our pals, Al Dodge, had traded Robert some rare records in exchange for a drawing of a large jazz band made up entirely of cats playing all the instruments of the orchestra. Every time I went over to Al's house I admired that drawing. A few years later, I found a copy of a rare Okeh Records 78 by Freeney's Barn Dance Band. Robert wanted the record badly, so I offered to trade it for a drawing like the one he'd done for Al. Not wanting to slave over drawing a twelve-piece orchestra again, he suggested a string band trio instead. I agreed, on the condition that he would color it as well, and the resultant portrait of Dirty Dog and the Smelly Old Cat Bros. String Band is still hanging in my record room today. It looks like the forerunner to the depictions of old bands included here.

The portraits of musicians that make up this book were drawn around 1980 with the idea that they would be reduced in size and printed as trading cards. Robert drew the musicians from existing studio and family photographs, but (even though he was quite fascinated with old photographs) I think he was more inspired by a love of the music on the 78s than he was by the photos themselves. In those days, Robert and I were well acquainted with Nick Perls, who owned and operated Yazoo Records in New York. Nick probably had the best collection in the world of original prewar blues 78s. He reissued them on LP compilations in a slow but steady labor of love, a labor that has continued after his death by Shanachie Records and his old friend Richard Nevins.

Robert's original idea was to include a single music card with each Yazoo LP, in much the same spirit as the established trading card tradition that dates back over a century. Packages of tobacco used to have card inserts that featured film, sports, and war subjects. When we were kids in the 1950s, trading cards were more likely found in a pack of gum. Over time, you could amass a collection of these cards. Inevitably, you'd realize that one or two rare ones were missing from your collection and you could either buy more gum in the hope of finding the cards you needed, or — worse — be forced to deal with the extortion of some rival collector who already owned the card you desired.

It was Nick Perls who wanted to package the cards as a thirty-six-piece boxed set. That eliminated the trading aspect, but gave Nick an additional item to sell rather than a bonus premium to give away with his paltry LP sales. He also had Robert design beautiful point-of-purchase store displays for the card sets, which are rare and collectible items today. I remember walking around the West Village with Nick as he tried to talk the local merchants into carrying the card sets. He was pretty successful. The cards were appealing and colorful and sold well right from the start. Numerous printings were done over the years, and the rights passed from Nick to other publishers. After Nick died, the original artwork for the cards was sold and today is owned by a successful film director in northern California. (No, not me.)

Initially, Robert wanted to draw only country string bands for the country set, but he was persuaded to include Jimmie Rodgers, the Carter Family, and a few more well-known entertainers. Robert liked these artists, but he seemed to get a bigger kick out of celebrating the lesser-known bands. Perhaps he wanted to give them a well-deserved bit of recognition after all their years of obscurity. The existence of available photographs partly determined the musicians he chose to include. It's a minor miracle that someone had a photo of Mumford Bean and His Itawambians, a band so obscure that their one existing 78 has only been heard by maybe a dozen hard-core country collectors, and has never been reissued.

As I recall, the blues and country sets were drawn first. I remember walking with Robert to Flax Art Supply on Market Street in San Francisco, where he bought the Pantone sheets he used to color them. He switched to watercolors and actually painted the jazz cards. I would like to wax eloquent here and impress the reader by attributing Robert's shift to painting the jazz cards to something about the fluidity inherent in the nature of jazz or some such nonsense, but I truly don't think that's the case. He probably switched to watercolors because he was tired of painstakingly cutting out that Pantone with an X-Acto knife all day.

As evocative as the artwork in this book is, the only way to really get at what has inspired the artist is to listen to the music — the inclusion here of a twenty-one track CD of some of the bands represented in this book is a good start. I would highly recommend Yazoo Records and also County Records as two of the best and most trusted resources available for more music of this period.

**Terry Zwigoff** is the director of *Crumb* (1994) — winner of the Grand Jury Prize at the Sundance Film Festival, as well as Best Documentary from the New York Film Critics Circle, the Los Angeles Film Critics Association, the National Society of Film Critics, and the Directors Guild of America. The documentary appeared on more than 150 Top Ten Best Films of the Year lists. His other movies include *Louie Bluie* (1985); *Ghost World* (2001) — for which he was nominated for an Academy Award (along with cowriter Daniel Clowes for Best Screenplay); *Bad Santa* (2003); and *Art School Confidential* (2006).

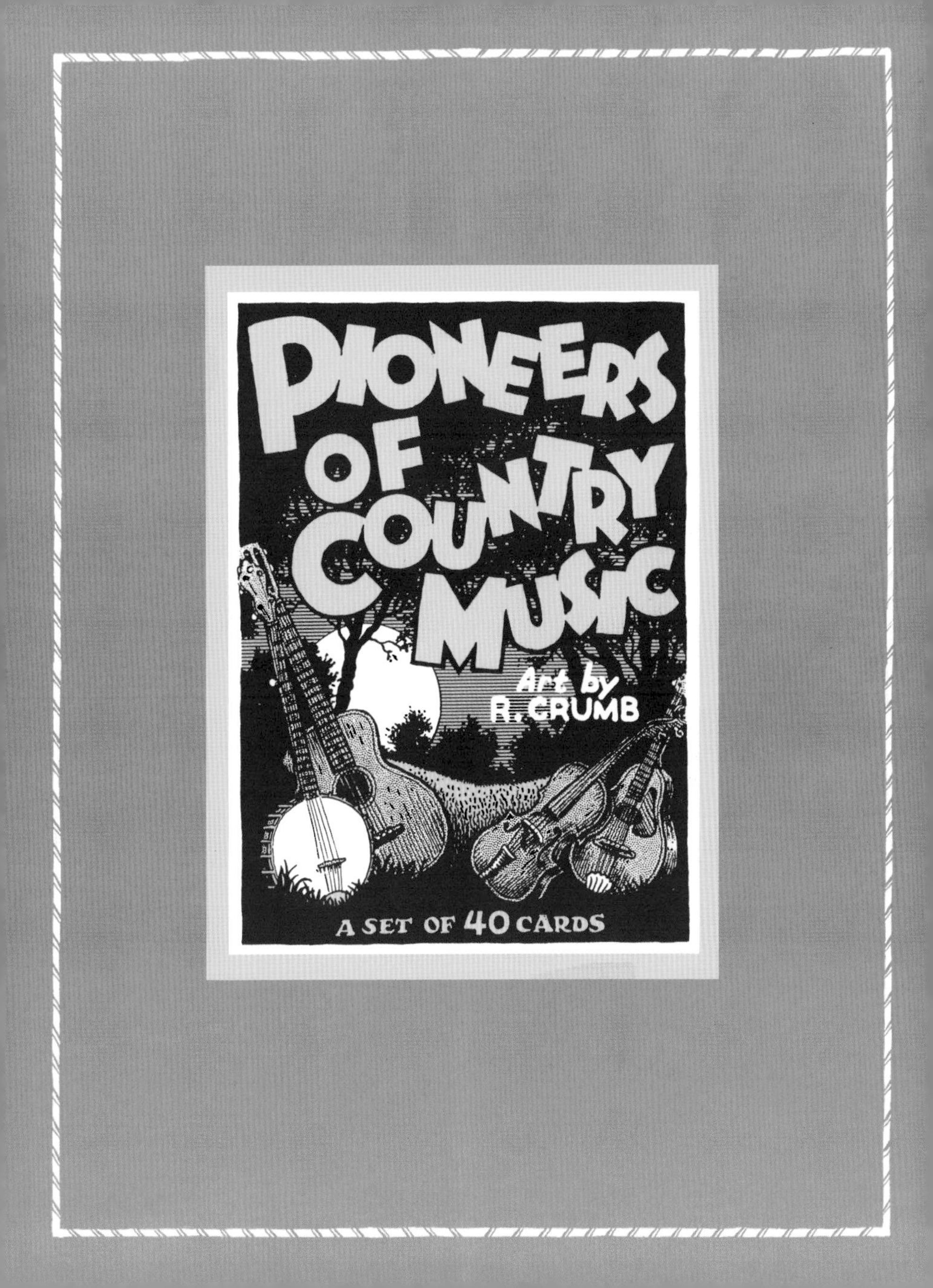
PIONEERS OF COUNTRY MUSIC
Art by R. CRUMB
A SET OF 40 CARDS

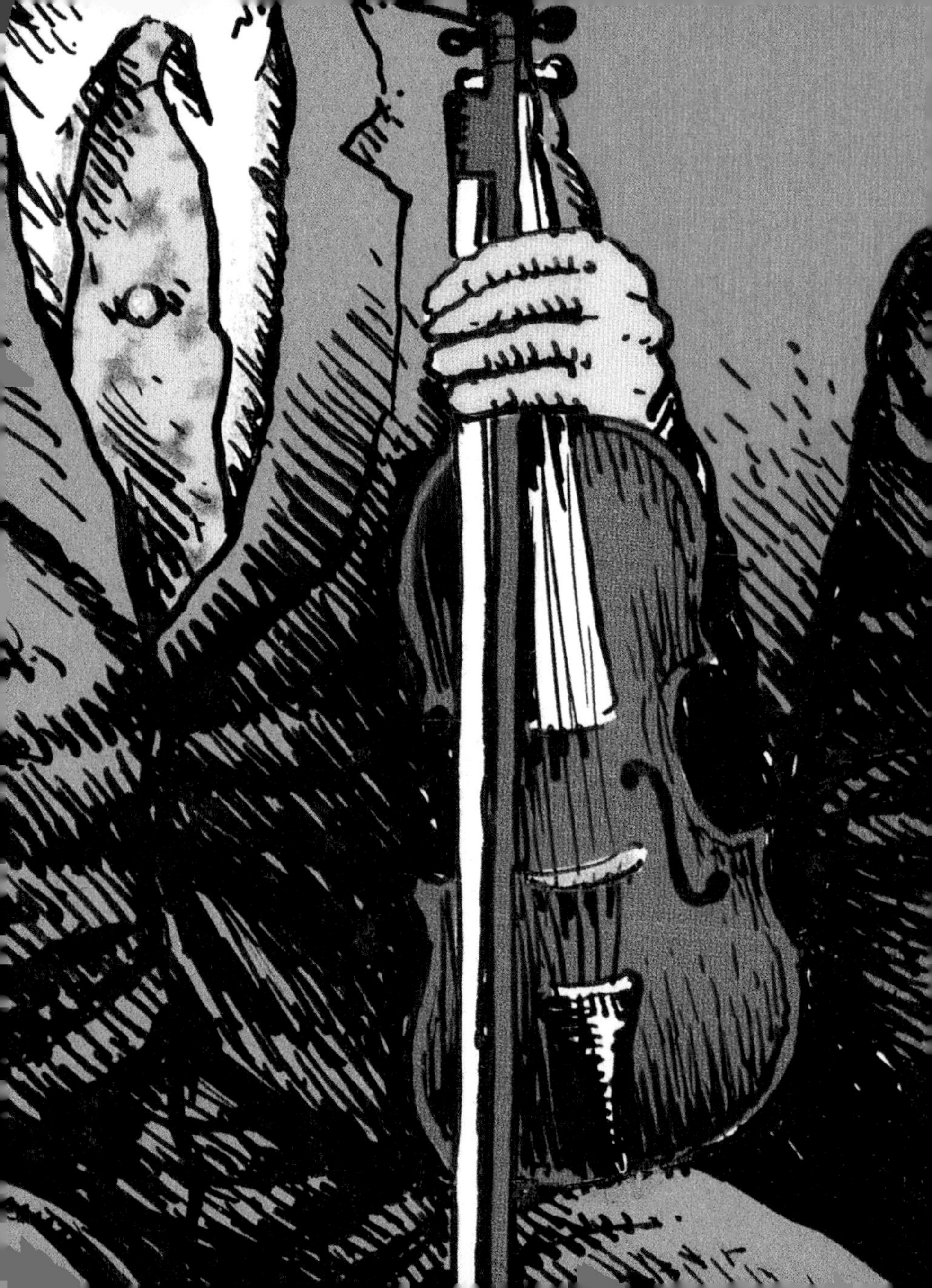

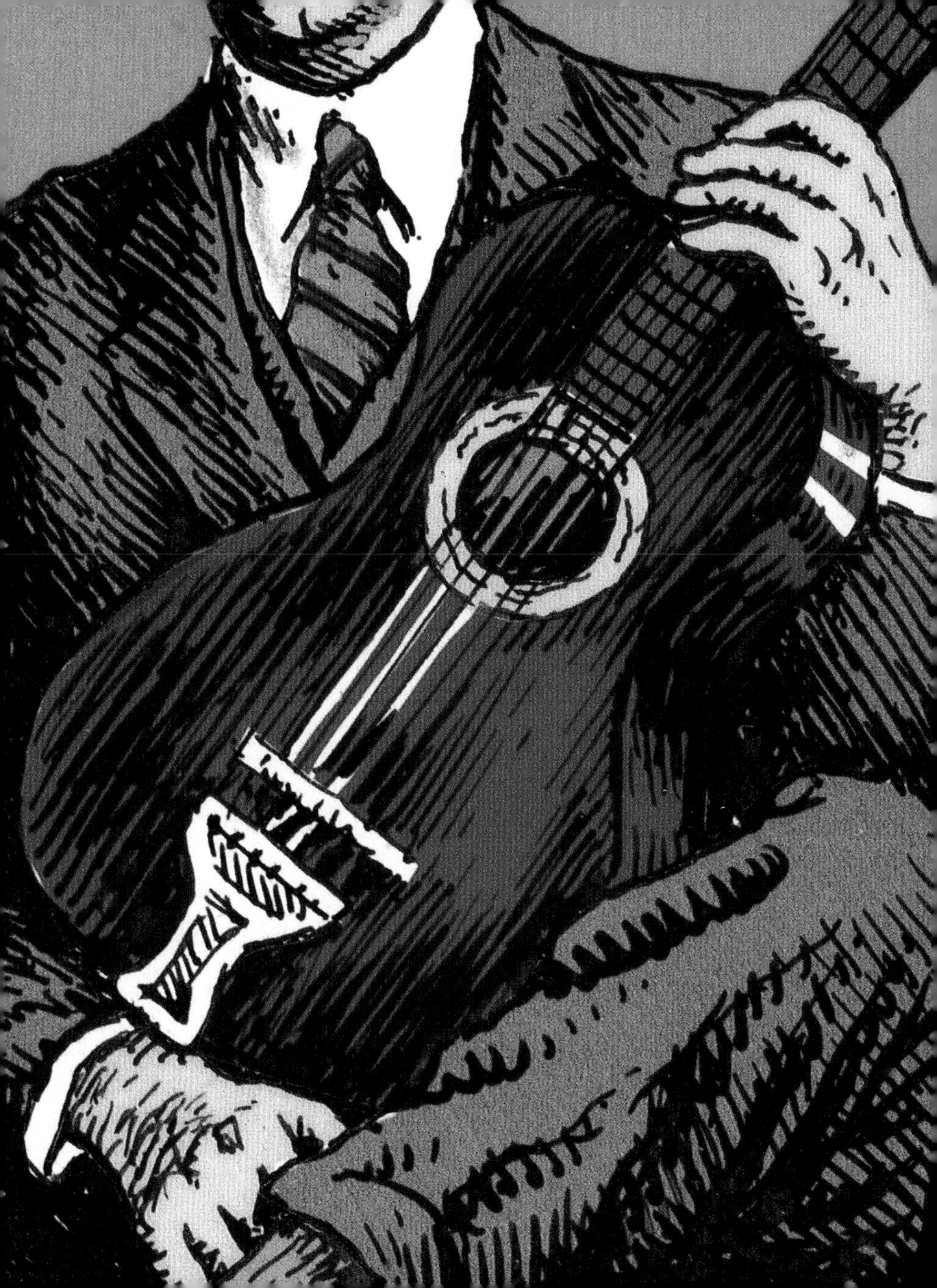

# WILLIAM MOORE

*B: Georgia, March 3, 1893*
*D: November 22, 1951*

A barber by trade, William Moore was born in Georgia in 1893 and spent most of his life in Tappahannock, Virginia. His eight extant sides, recorded at a single Paramount Records session in 1928, stamp him as one of the few instrumentally oriented performers of the era. Moore's upbeat music may echo the happy-go-lucky ragtime dances popular before the heyday of the blues. "Ragtime Millionaire" is probably his best-known song.

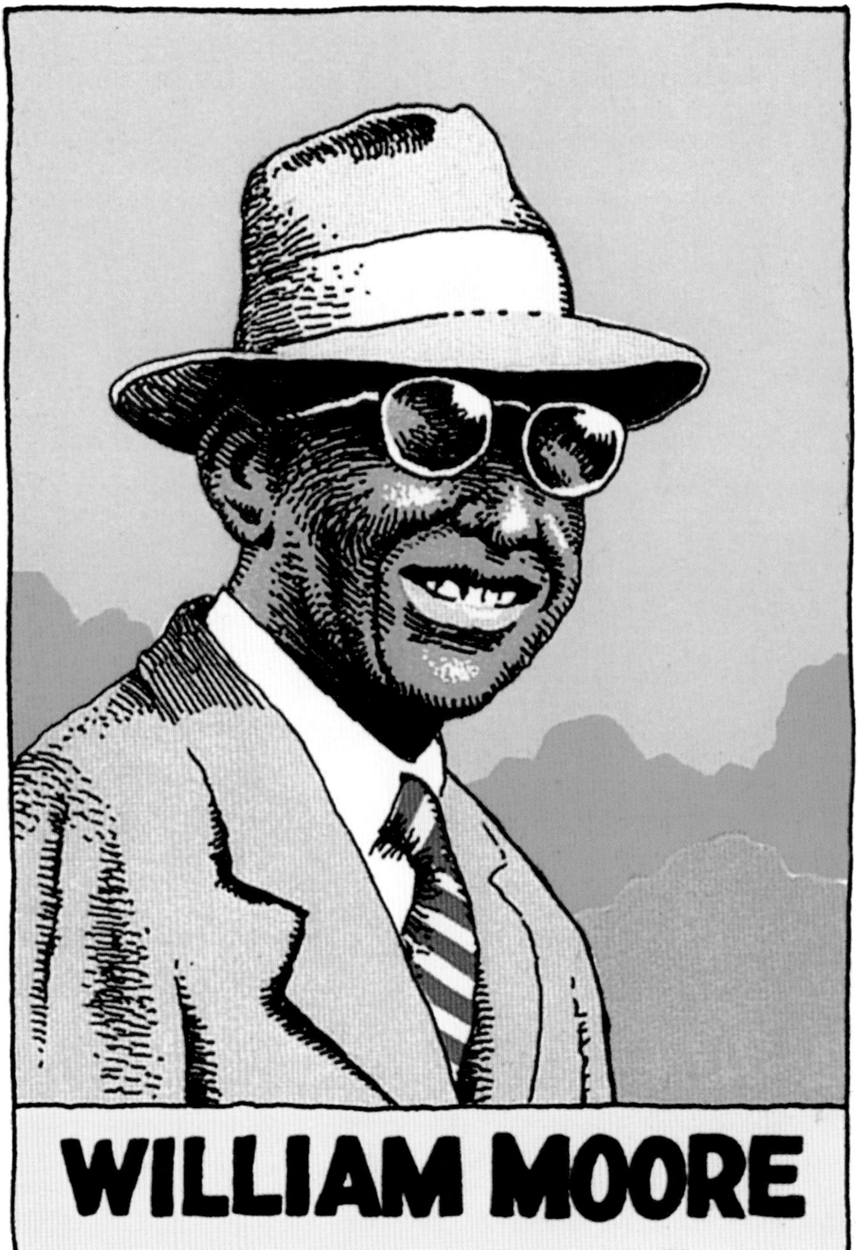
WILLIAM MOORE

# PEG LEG HOWELL

*B: Eatonton, Georgia, March 3, 1888*
*D: Atlanta, Georgia, August 11, 1966*

A native of Eatonton, Georgia, Joshua Barnes "Peg Leg" Howell taught himself guitar around 1909, at the age of twenty-one, and subsequently worked in Atlanta as a street singer. Howell was one of the earliest country blues performers to be recorded. He made twenty-eight sides, many with string band accompaniment, between 1926 and 1929. Like most street singers of the period, Howell had a diverse repertoire that included both blues and up-tempo ragtime songs.

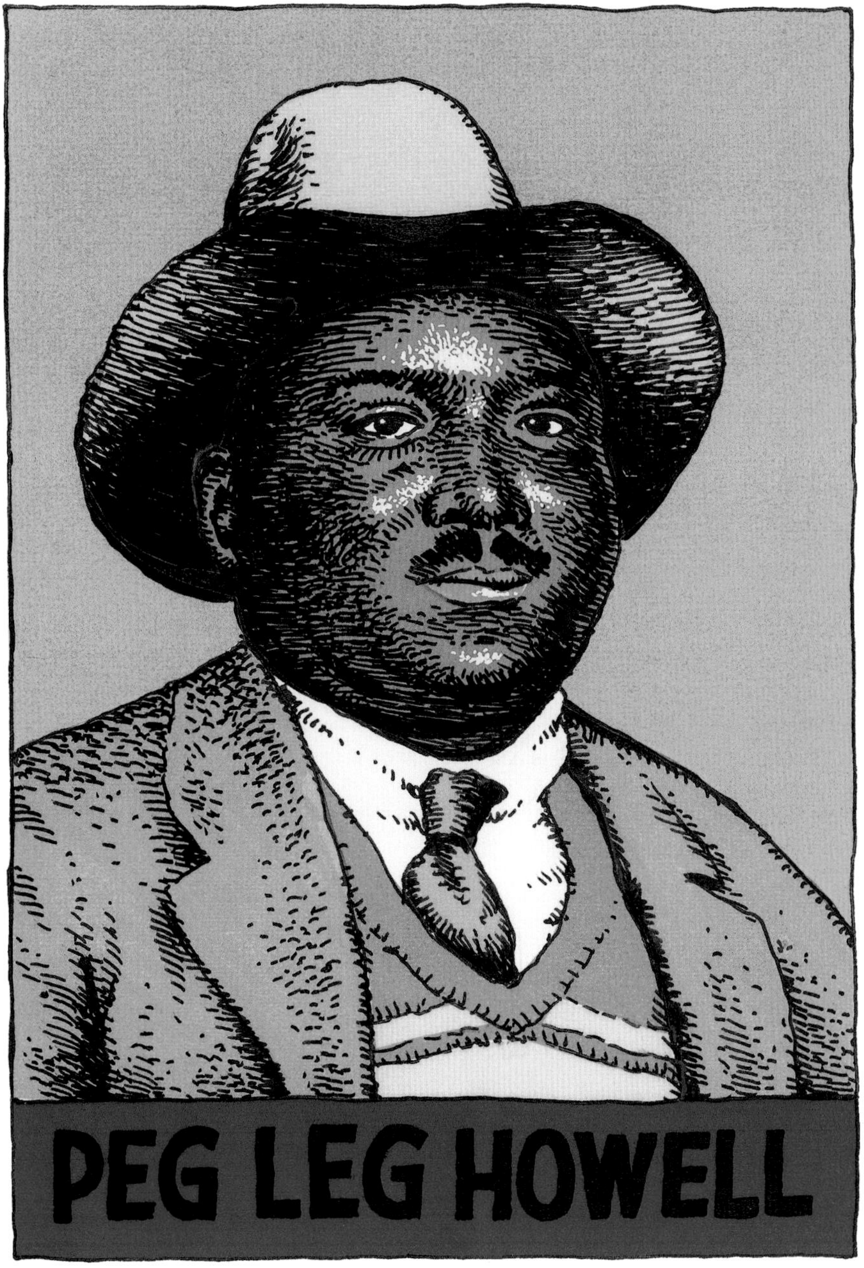

PEG LEG HOWELL

# CLIFFORD GIBSON

*B: Louisville, Kentucky, April 17, 1901*
*D: St. Louis, Missouri, December 21, 1963*

Born in Louisville, Kentucky, in 1901, Clifford Gibson cut his musical teeth in St. Louis. He recorded twenty-four sides for two different labels between 1929 and 1931. One of the first purely urban performers whose playing had no pronounced rural influences, Gibson's single-string, vibrato-laden approach resembled that of the highly sophisticated jazz blues guitarist Lonnie Johnson, but placed more emphasis on improvisation.

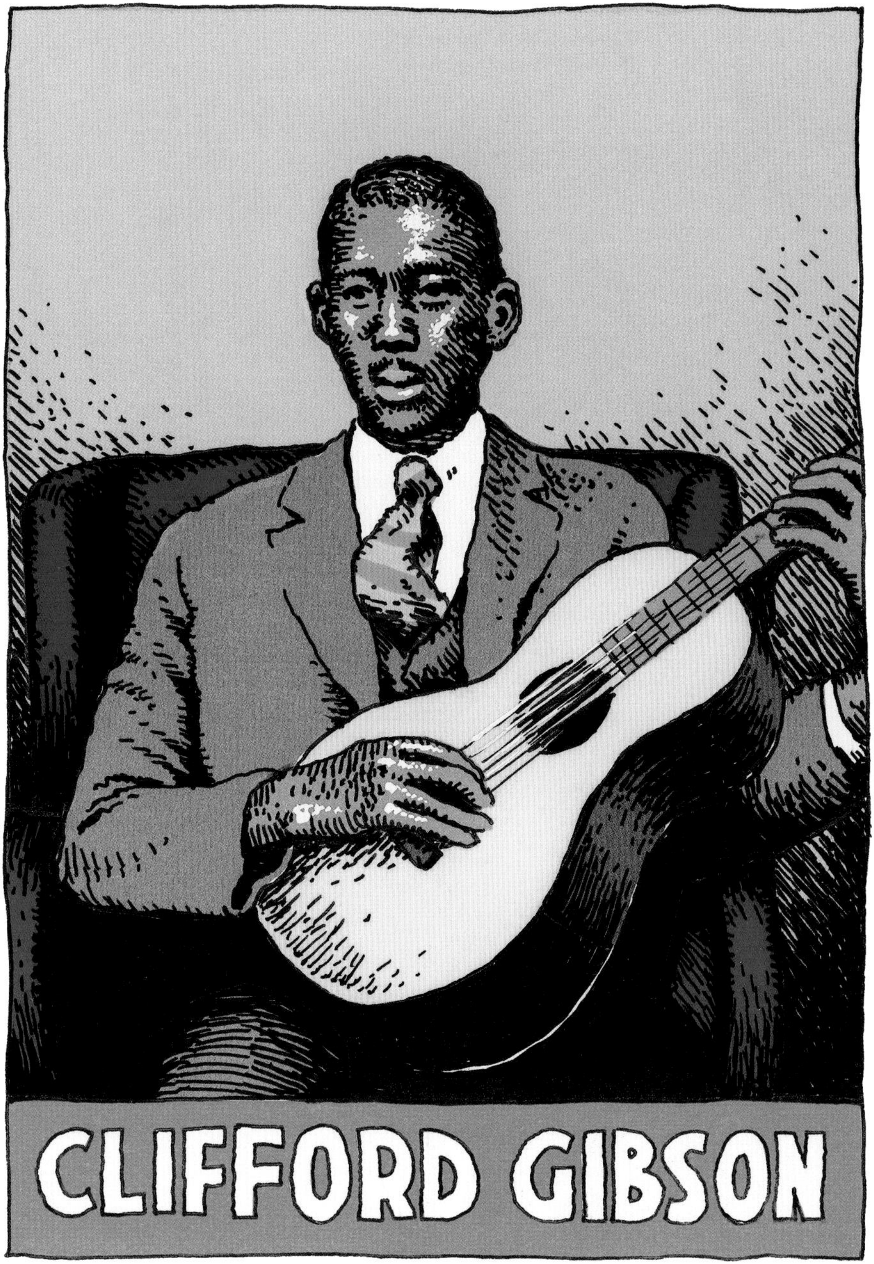
CLIFFORD GIBSON

# BLIND BLAKE

B: *Jacksonville, Florida, 1895*
D: *Jacksonville, Florida, 1937*

Jacksonville's Arthur "Blind" Blake ranks among the most accomplished rag and blues guitarists of all time. In the 1920s he based his career in Chicago. Between 1926 and 1932 he recorded nearly eighty sides for Paramount Records, afterward fading into obscurity. Unlike many blind blues performers, Blake played up-tempo dance-oriented music. His polished technique and effortless-sounding improvisations attracted many imitators, but admitted no equals.

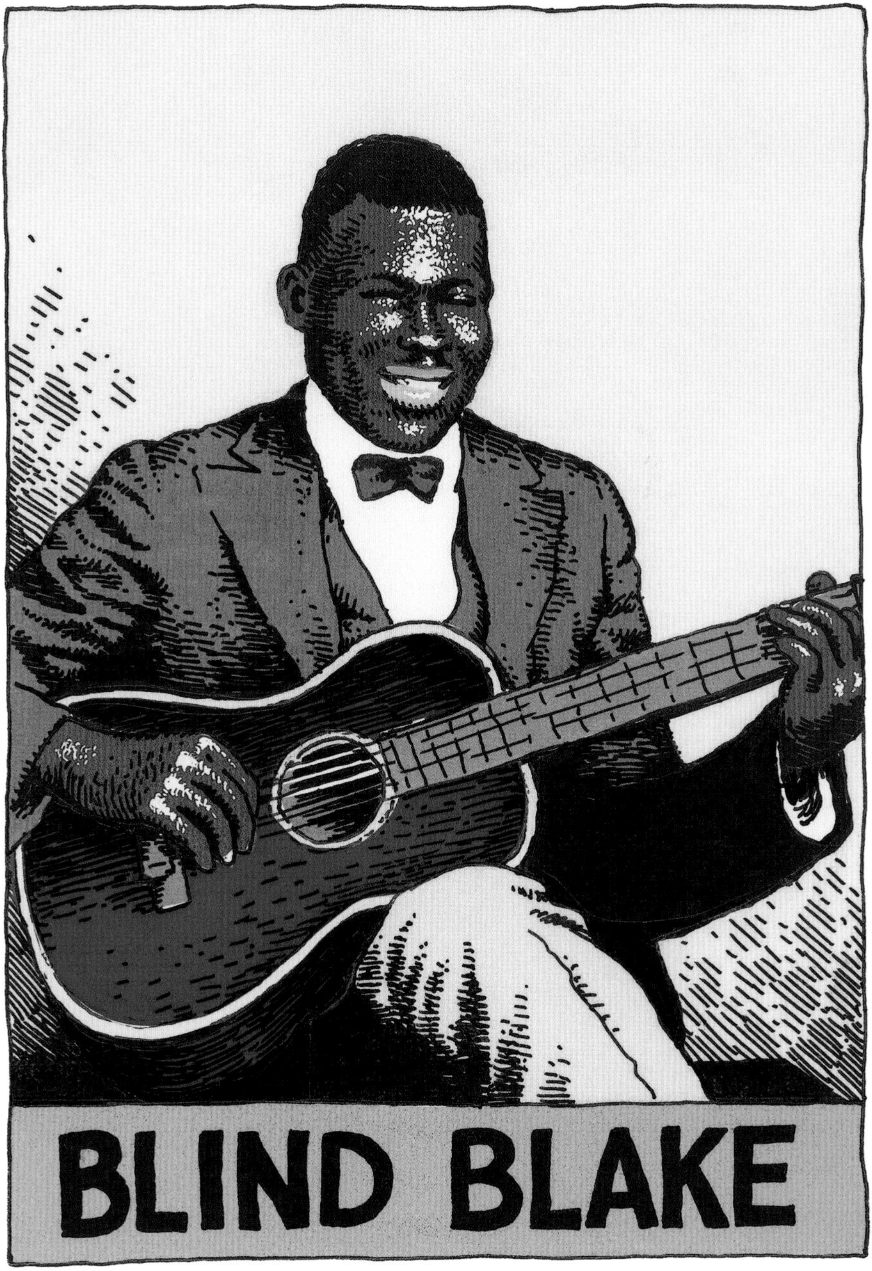
BLIND BLAKE

# FRANK STOKES

*B: Whitehaven, Tennessee, January 1, 1888*
*D: Memphis, Tennessee, September 12, 1955*

Born in 1888 in Whitehaven, Tennessee, Frank Stokes began playing around 1900, and pursued his career in Memphis, where he became one of the city's most popular entertainers. Between 1927 and 1929 he recorded thirty-six sides for two labels, usually in tandem with his accompanist, Dan Sane. His best-known tune was "Crump Don't 'Low It," which referred to the mayor of Memphis and was nationally associated with composer W. C. Handy.

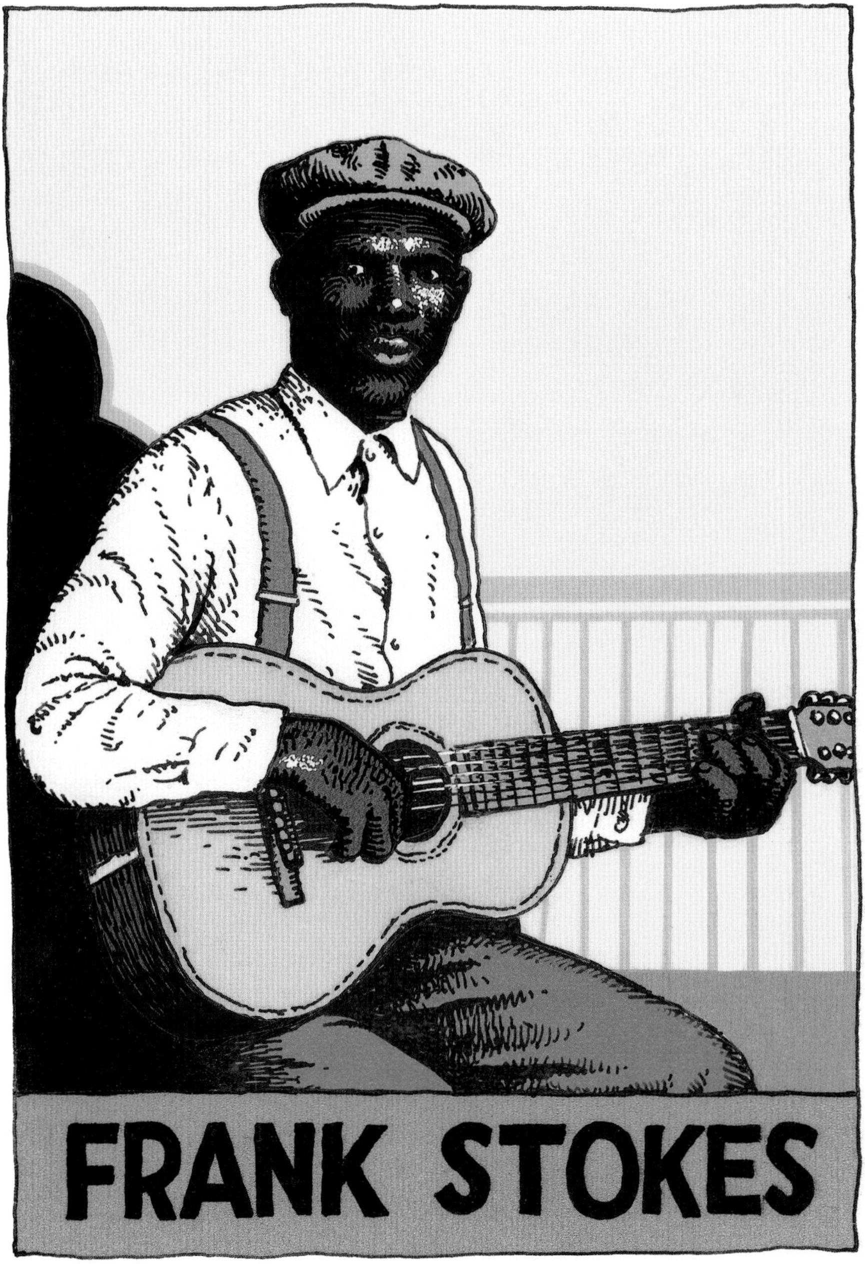
FRANK STOKES

# JAYBIRD COLEMAN

*B: Gainesville, Alabama, 1896*
*D: Tuskegee, Alabama, January 28, 1950*

Burl "Jaybird" Coleman was born in Gainesville, Alabama, in 1896 and began playing harmonica around 1908, settling in Bessemer in the early 1920s. Between 1927 and 1930 he made eleven sides, appearing in the rather unusual role of a harmonica player accompanying his own vocals. Of all recorded blues harmonica players, Coleman developed probably the richest and most varied tone. He was largely inactive after 1930, and died in 1950.

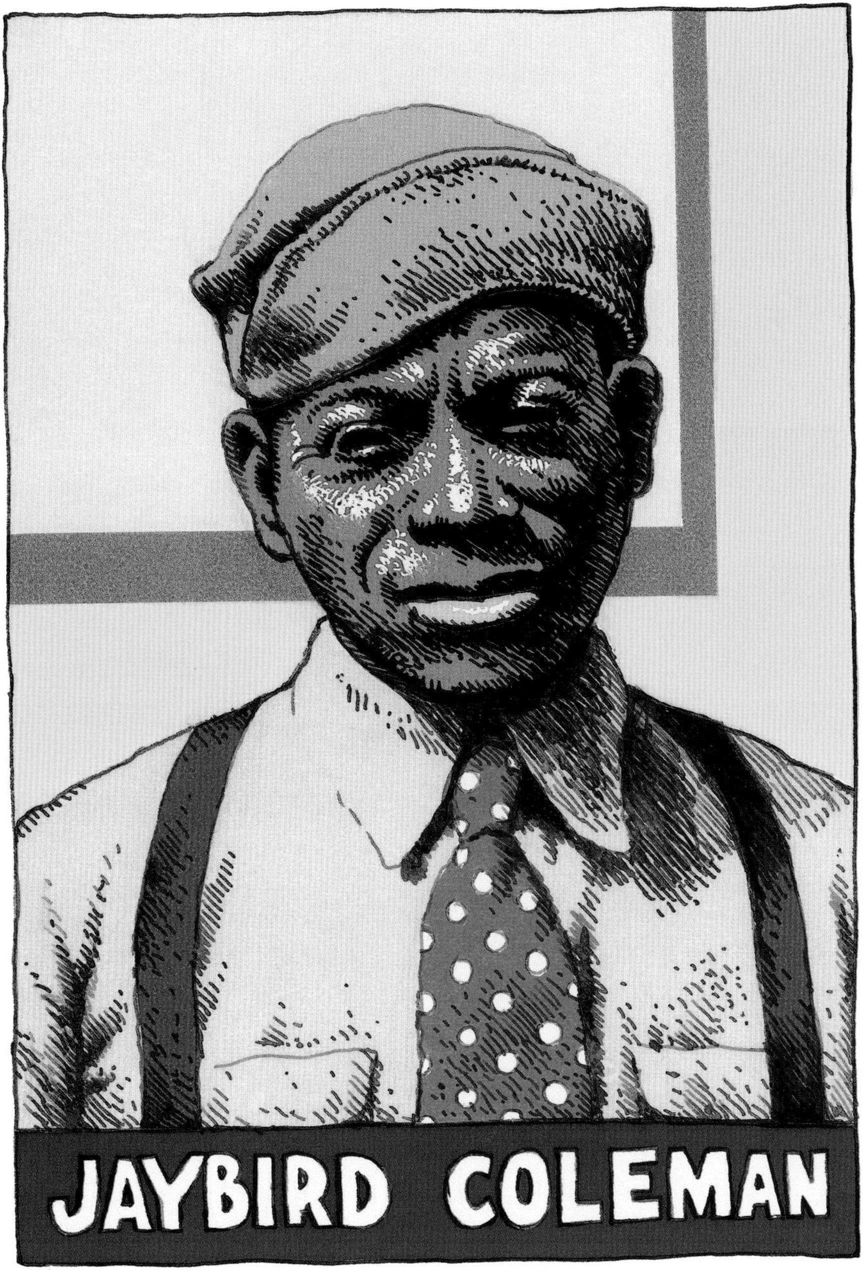
JAYBIRD COLEMAN

# BLIND WILLIE JOHNSON

*B: Marlin, Texas, 1902*
*D: Beaumont, Texas, 1947*

A native of Marlin, Texas, Blind Willie Johnson worked
as a gospel singer. Between 1927 and 1930 he recorded
thirty sides, including several vocal duets with his
wife. Although religious in orientation, Johnson's music
was as percussive as any dance blues, and he attained
the most rhythmically fluid and tonally vibrant sound of
any bottleneck guitarist of his time. His best-known
piece is probably "Dark Was the Night (Cold Was the
Ground)." He died in 1947 in Beaumont, Texas.

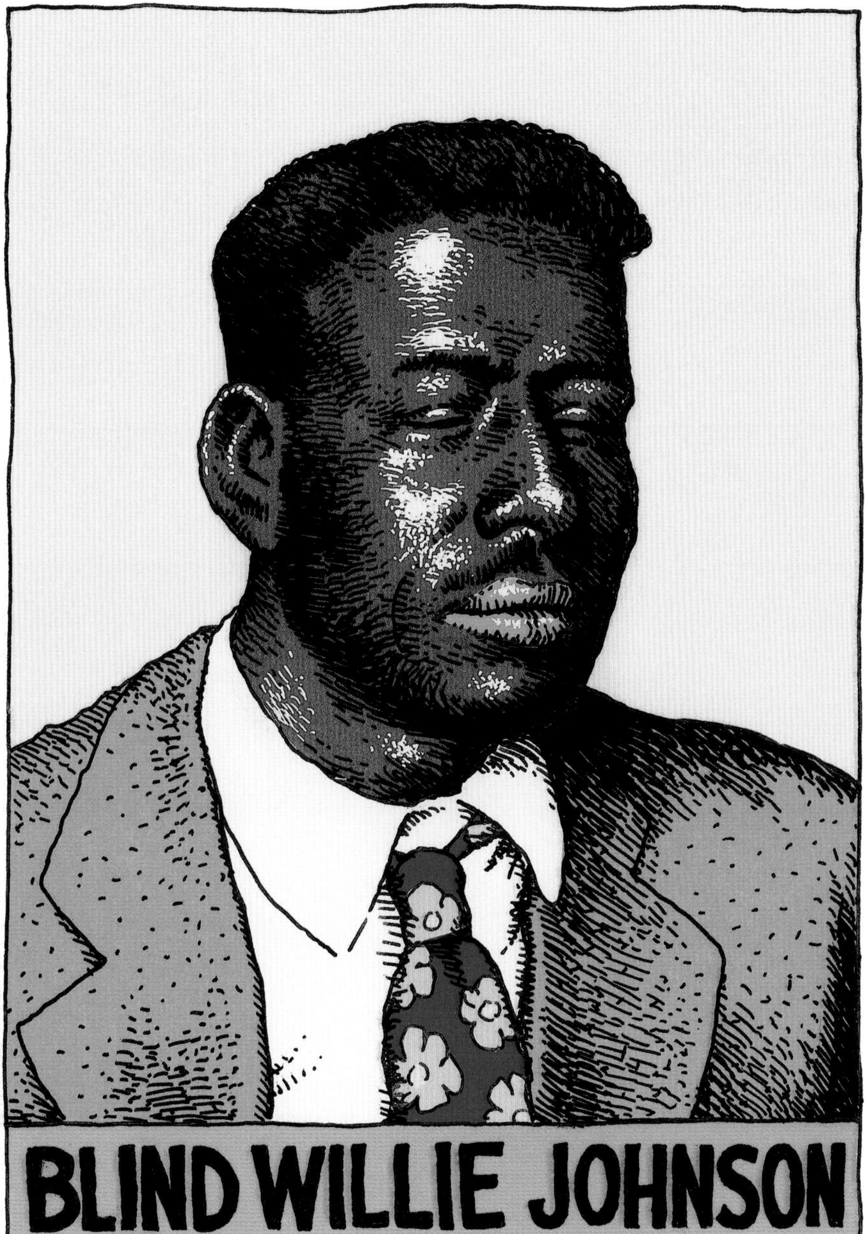
BLIND WILLIE JOHNSON

# LEROY CARR

*B: Nashville, Tennessee, March 27, 1905*
*D: Indianapolis, Indiana, April 29, 1935*

# SCRAPPER BLACKWELL

*B: Syracuse, South Carolina, February 21, 1903*
*D: Indianapolis, Indiana, October 1962*

Leroy Carr, one of the first blues singers to use an understated vocal delivery, was born in Nashville in 1905. Francis "Scrapper" Blackwell was born in 1903 and learned guitar in childhood, eventually developing a delicate vibrato blended with string-snapping. The Indianapolis-based team of Carr and Blackwell popularized the piano-guitar blues duet. They made more than one hundred sides between 1928 and Carr's death in 1935, including the famous "How Long Blues."

LEROY CARR and SCRAPPER BLACKWELL

# BLIND LEMON JEFFERSON

*B: Couchman, Texas, September 1893*
*D: Chicago, Illinois, December 1929*

A native of Couchman, Texas, near Wortham, the
legendary Blind Lemon Jefferson worked as a street
singer and visited several states in the course of his
travels. His successful recording debut in 1926 launched
the vogue for country blues. Before his mysterious
death in 1929, Jefferson recorded eighty-five sides and
established himself as the most popular blues guitarist
of his era. An offbeat guitarist known for his free
phrasing patterns, he was one of the most inspired
singers found in blues.

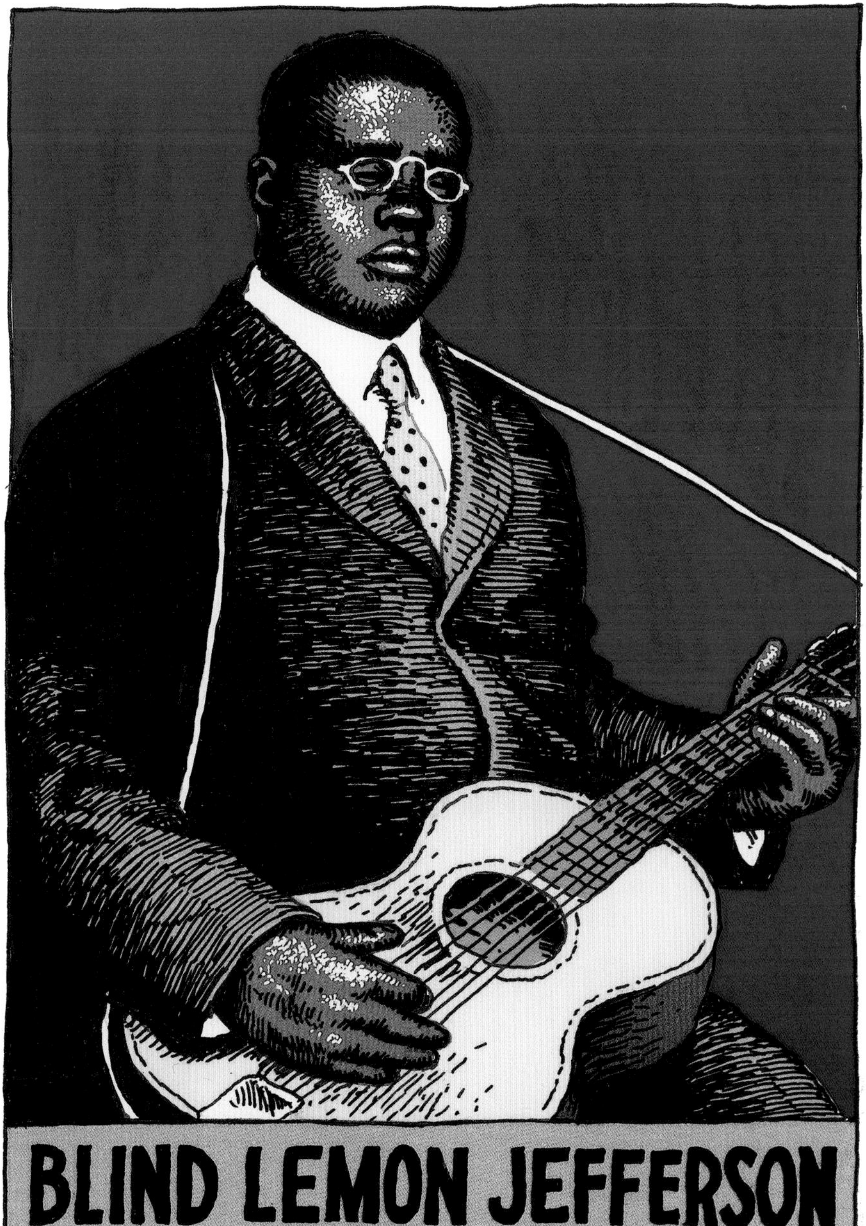
BLIND LEMON JEFFERSON

# CURLEY WEAVER

*B: Covington, Georgia, March 26, 1906*
*D: Atlanta, Georgia, September 20, 1962*

# FRED McMULLEN

*B: Unknown*
*D: Unknown*

Curley Weaver was born in 1906 and raised near Porterdale, Georgia. He learned guitar around 1922 and moved to Atlanta a few years later. Most of his records were duets with other local blues recording artists, such as Atlanta–based Blind Willie McTell and Fred McMullen of Macon, Georgia. McMullen began recording in 1933. He teamed up with Weaver and Buddy Moss that same year in a recording trio known as the Georgia Browns.

**CURLEY WEAVER** and **FRED McMULLEN**

# WHISTLER & HIS JUG BAND

The first jug band to record was Whistler & His Jug Band, a group hailing from the Louisville, Kentucky, area where, beginning at the turn of the century, jug bands playing string band arrangements entertained during the Kentucky Derby. From 1924 to 1931 Whistler's aggregation recorded twenty-one titles for three different companies. A movie clip of the essentially unknown players exists, a still from which provided the source for this illustration.

WHISTLER & HIS JUG BAND

# MISSISSIPPI SHEIKS

| **Walter Vinson** | **Lonnie Chatmon** | **Bo Carter** |
|---|---|---|
| B: *Bolton, Mississippi, February 2, 1901* | B: *Unknown* | B: *Bolton, Mississippi, March 21, 1893* |
| D: *Chicago, Illinois, 1975* | D: *Unknown* | D: *Memphis, Tennessee, September 21, 1964* |

Singer-guitarist Walter Vinson and fiddler Lonnie Chatmon worked together for more than a decade before recording as the Mississippi Sheiks in 1930 and producing the hit "Sitting on Top of the World." Natives of Bolton, Mississippi, they played for local white square dances, often with Chatmon's brothers, who included Bo Carter (Armenter Chatmon), seen here on the left (and on page 87). Both read music, and their seventy-eight titles offer a mixture of blues and pop styles. They disbanded soon after their final session in 1935.

MISSISSIPPI SHEIKS

# RUBE LACEY

: *Pelahatchie, Mississippi, January 2, 1901*
: *California, 1972*

Rubin "Rube" Lacey was born in 1901 at Pelahatchie, Mississippi, and learned guitar in his teens from an older performer, George Hendrix. Working out of the Jackson area in the Mississippi Delta, he became one of the state's most popular blues singers. His bottleneck style inspired that of the better-known performer Son House. In 1928 Lacey recorded two dance tunes for Paramount Records; four years later he became a minister.

BLUES

• 40 •

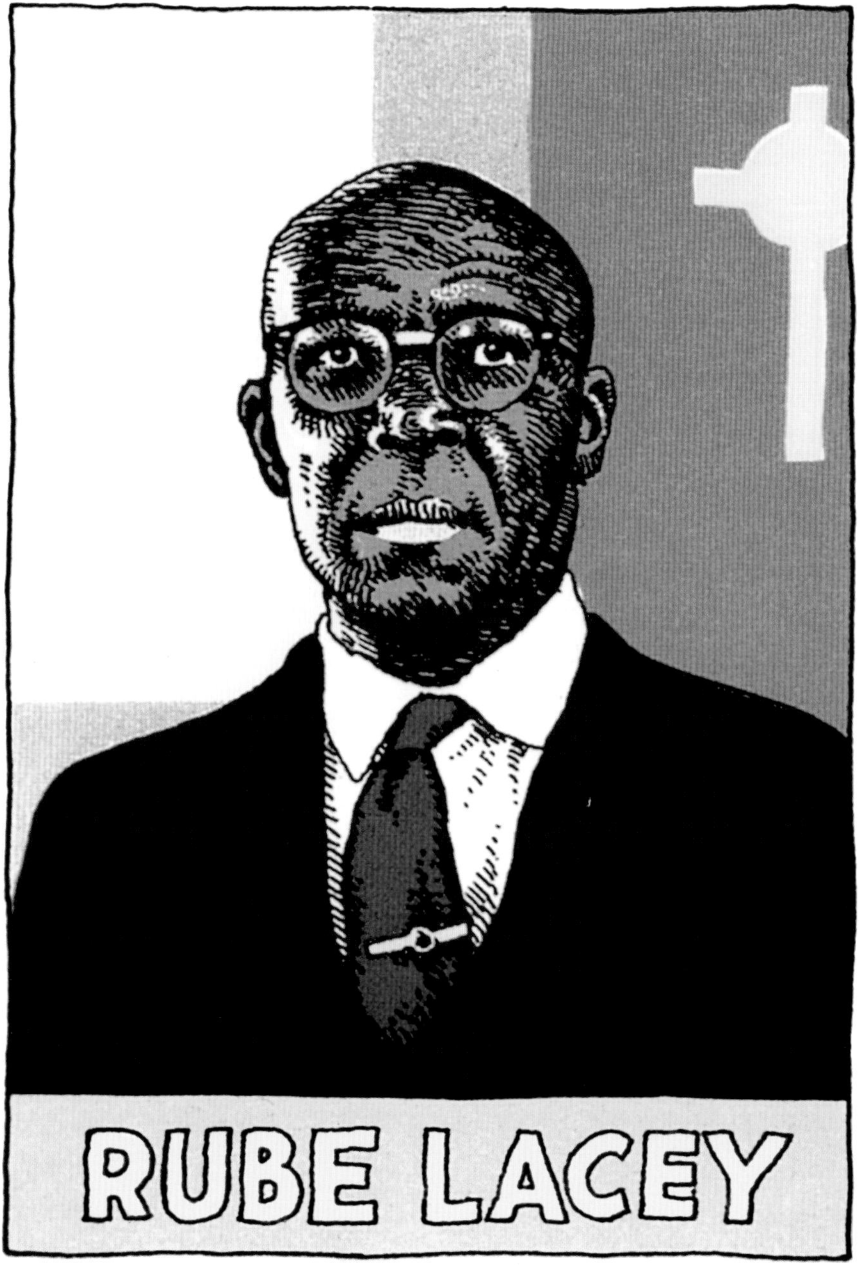
RUBE LACEY

# SKIP JAMES

*B: Bentonia, Mississippi, June 9, 1902*
*D: Philadelphia, Pennsylvania, October 3, 1969*

Nehemiah "Skip" James was born in 1902 and raised
in Bentonia, Mississippi. He learned guitar in his late
teens from a local player, Henry Stuckey, and began
piano soon afterward under the tutelage of an older
Arkansas performer, Will Crabtree. A professional blues
musician from 1924 onward, James recorded seventeen
sides for Paramount Records in 1931, and entered the
clergy the same year. His "I'm So Glad" became a rock
hit by Cream shortly before his death in 1969.

SKIP JAMES

# BO-WEAVIL JACKSON

*B: Vicinity of Birmingham, Alabama*
*D: Unknown*

One of the earliest country blues performers to be
recorded, James "Bo-Weavil" Jackson was discovered
while singing on a Birmingham, Alabama, street in 1926.
He produced twelve sides for two labels, one of which
billed him as Sam Butler. His frantic tempos, impromptu
guitar figures, and use of varied melodic lines within
single songs mark Jackson as one of the blues' most distinctive and least predictable performers. His "You Can't
Keep No Brown" is a frenetic bottleneck masterpiece.

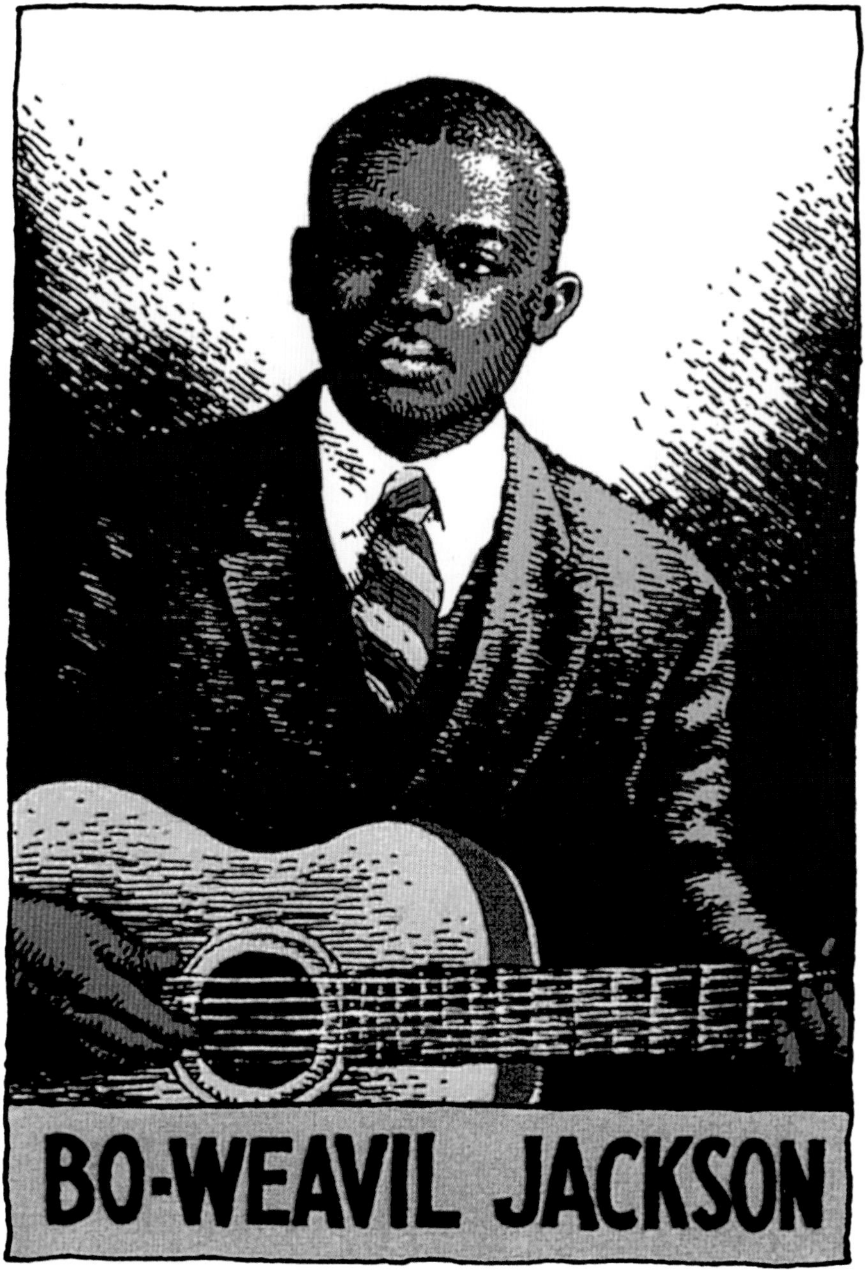
BO-WEAVIL JACKSON

# FURRY LEWIS

*B: Greenwood, Mississippi, March 6, 1899*
*D: Memphis, Tennessee, September 14, 1981*

Walter "Furry" Lewis was born in 1899 and raised in
Memphis, where he learned guitar in the early 1900s
by listening to a middle-aged street singer named Blind
Joe. Never a full-time musician, Lewis played mainly
on local streets, where his most popular piece was
"John Henry." From 1927 to 1928 he recorded twenty-
three sides. In the 1960s the personable Lewis began
a second career as a concert performer, even appearing
in the Burt Reynolds movie *W. W. and the Dixie
Dancekings* (1975).

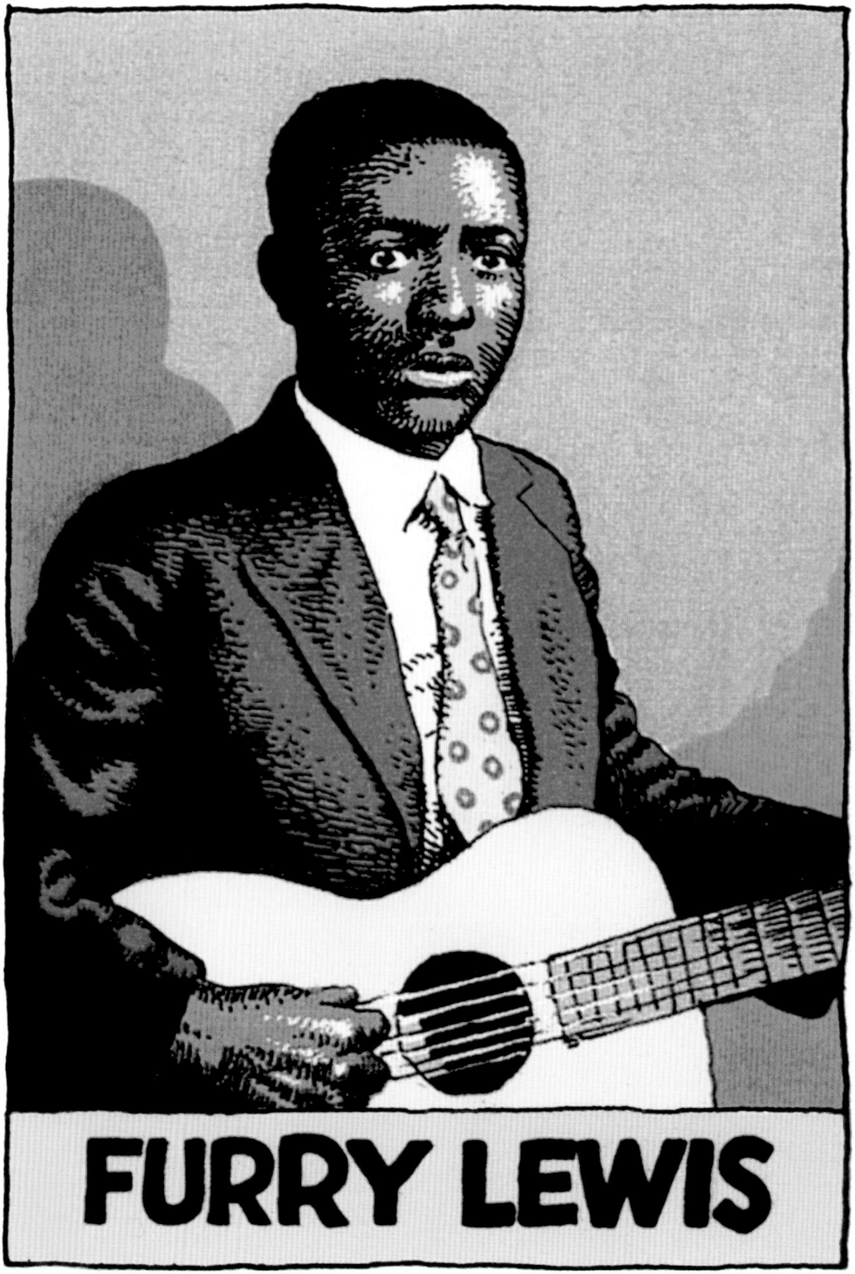
FURRY LEWIS

# SAM COLLINS

B: *Kentwood, Louisiana, August 11, 1887*
D: *Chicago, Illinois, October 20, 1949*

Born in 1887 in Louisiana, Sam Collins was raised in southern Mississippi. His nineteen extant recordings, made between 1927 and 1932, reflect a background in street singing and tent show musicianship similar to that of Georgia-born Blind Willie McTell. His free-form bottleneck guitar approach and his unusually high-pitched singing gave him a distinctive musical sound. Collins eventually settled in Chicago, where he died in 1949.

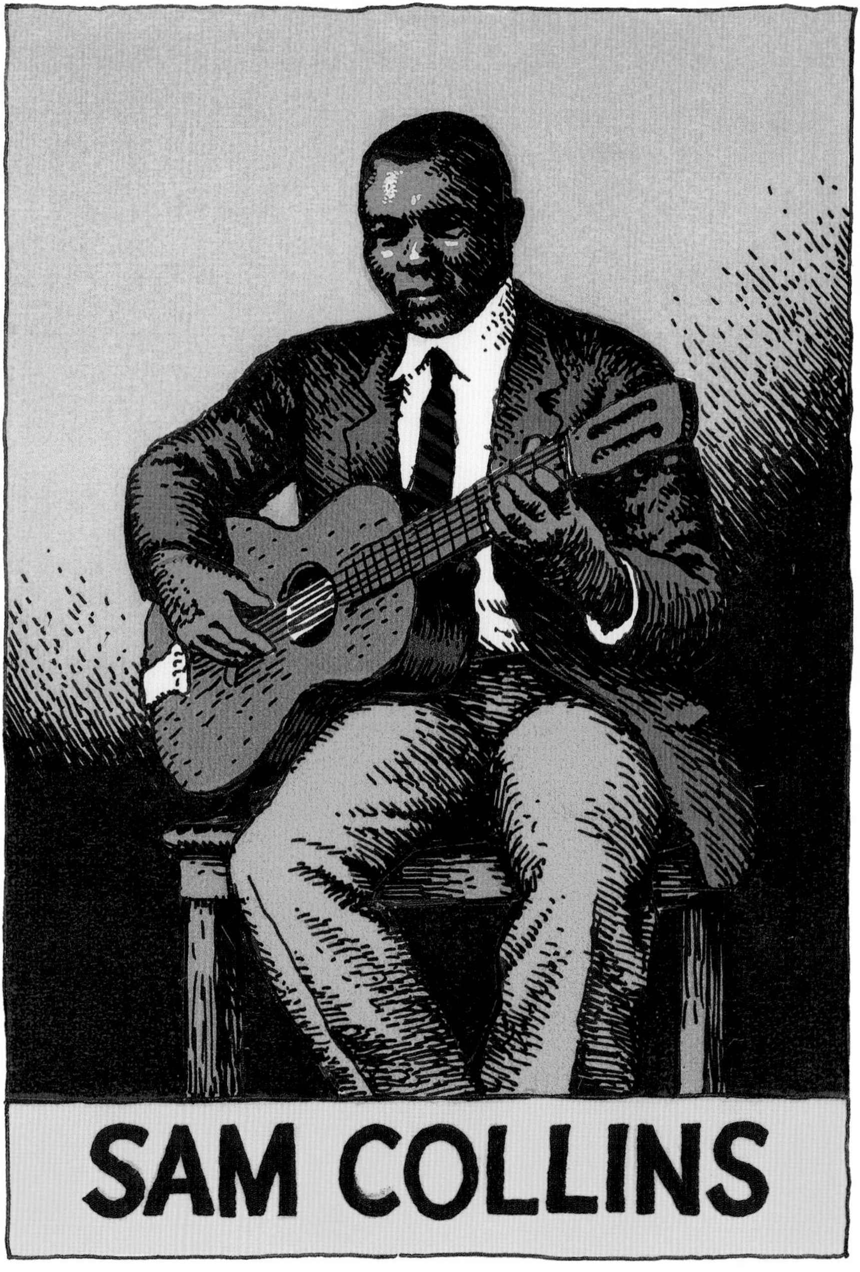
SAM COLLINS

# RAMBLIN' THOMAS

*B: Louisiana, 1902*
*D: Memphis, Tennessee, c. 1935*

Willard "Ramblin'" Thomas was born in 1902 and raised in Logansport, Louisiana. A self-taught guitarist, he played in Shreveport, Louisiana, and in Oklahoma before his discovery in Dallas. Between 1928 and 1932 he recorded eighteen sides, most of them in the idiom of a street performer. His colorful lyrics and free phrasing patterns invite comparison to Blind Lemon Jefferson. Thomas died in Memphis in the mid-1930s and was survived by his blues-playing brother, Babyface Thomas.

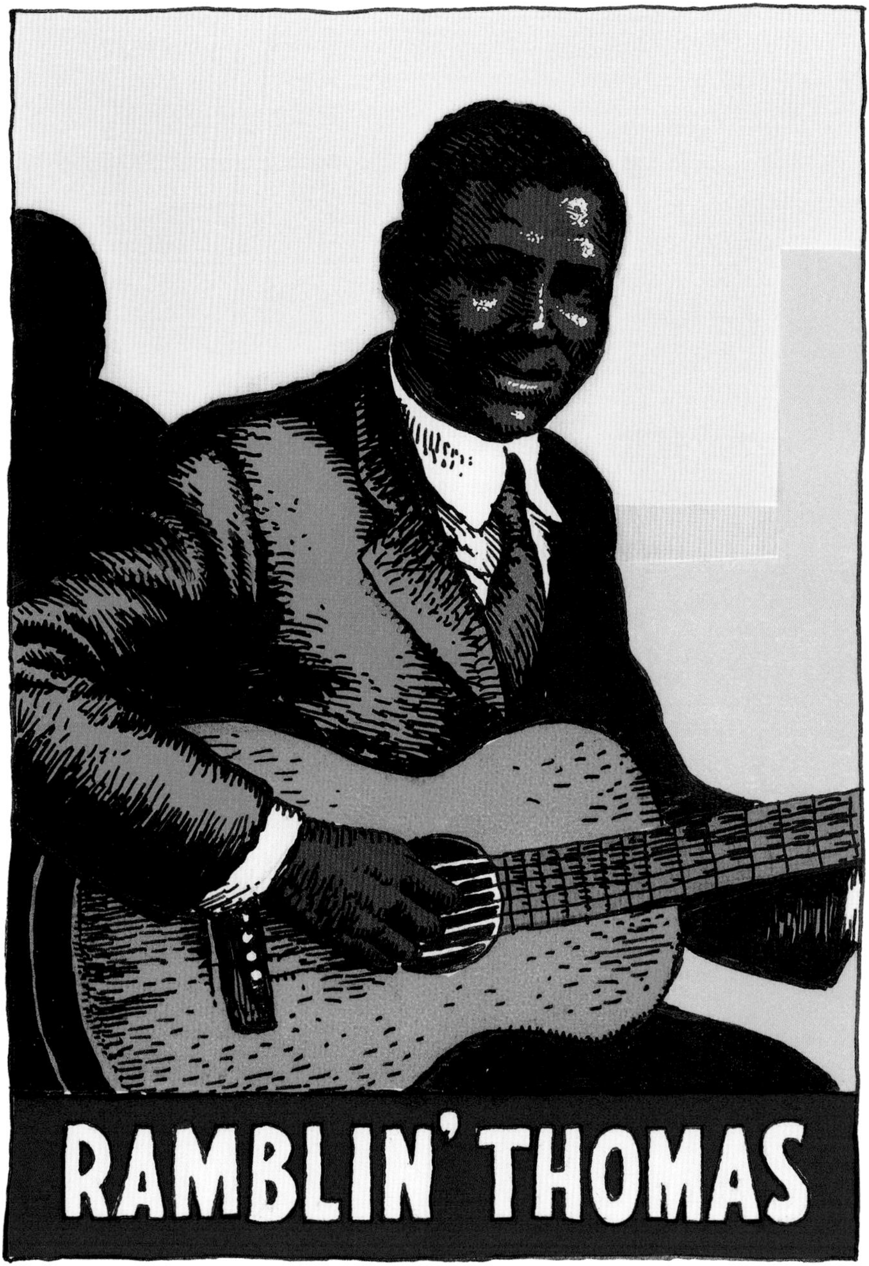
RAMBLIN' THOMAS

# SLEEPY JOHN ESTES

*B: Ripley, Tennessee, January 25, 1904*
*D: June 5, 1977*

One of the blues' most expressive vocalists, John Estes was born in 1904 in Ripley, Tennessee. He later moved to his lifelong home of Brownsville, where he learned guitar from Hambone Willie Newbern. Between 1929 and 1941 he recorded fifty sides, generally in an ensemble format that marked a departure from the usual country blues vein. Estes's tunes were notable for their topical references to local people and events. His career revived during the 1960s and he died in 1977.

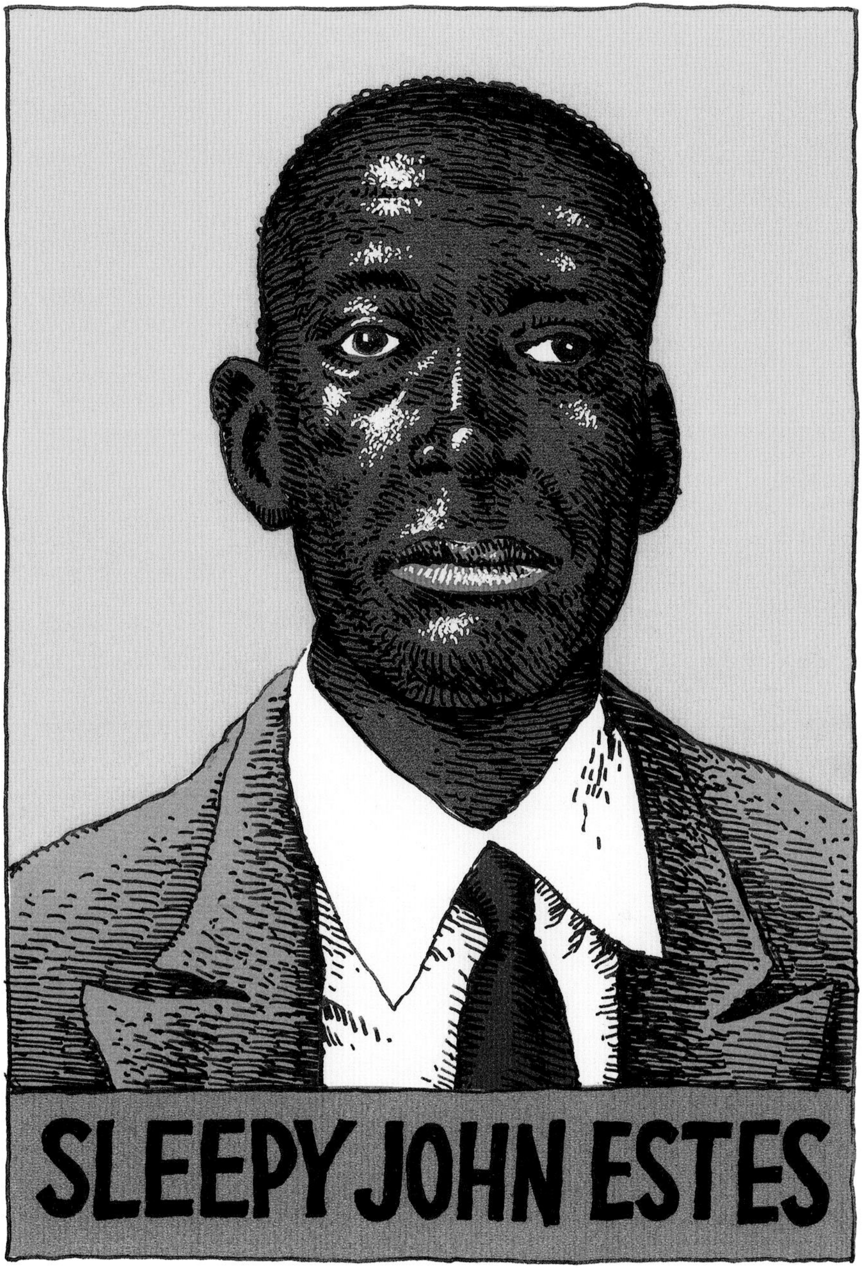
SLEEPY JOHN ESTES

# CANNON'S JUG STOMPERS

**Gus Cannon**
B: *Red Banks,*
*Mississippi,*
*September 12, 1883*
D: *October 15, 1979*

**Ashley Thompson**
B: *Unknown*
D: *Unknown*

**Noah Lewis**
B: *Henning, Tennessee,*
*September 3, 1895*
D: *Ripley, Tennessee,*
*February 7, 1961*

Cannon's Jug Stompers, based in Ripley, Tennessee, consisted of banjoist Gus Cannon ("Banjo Joe"), guitarist Ashley Thompson, and harmonicist Noah Lewis. Cannon was born in Mississippi in 1883 and played professionally before 1900. Lewis, a native of Henning, Tennessee, was born in 1895 and began working with Cannon around 1910. The group's twenty-eight recordings between 1928 and 1930 include "Walk Right In," made famous as a folk-rock song in the 1960s by the Rooftop Singers.

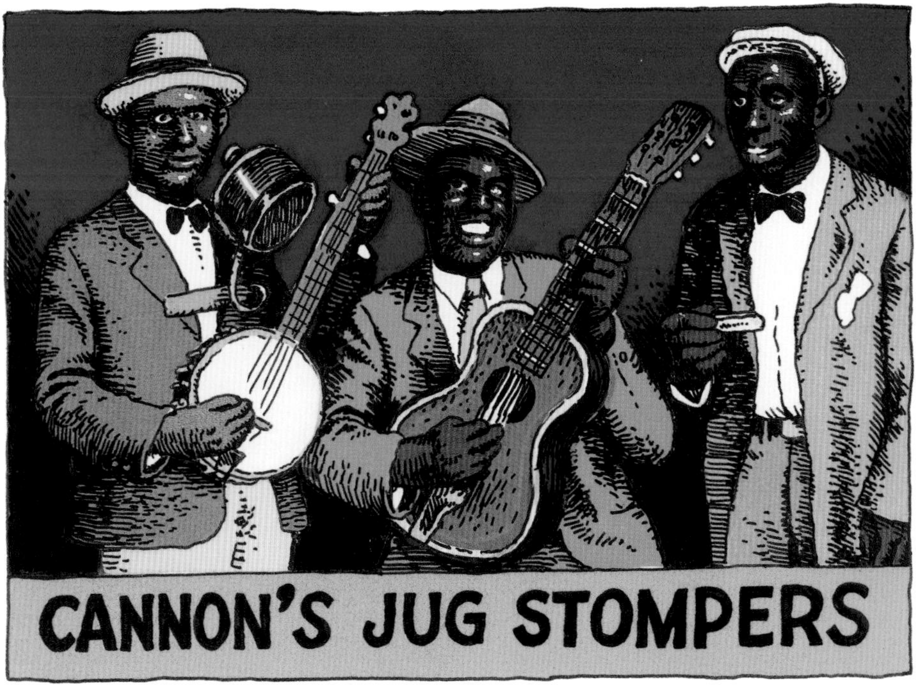
CANNON'S JUG STOMPERS

# MEMPHIS JUG BAND

| **Will Shade** | **Ben Ramey** | **Charles Polk** | **Will Weldon** |
| --- | --- | --- | --- |
| B: *Memphis, Tennessee, February 5, 1898* | B: *Unknown* | B: *Unknown* | B: *Unknown* |
| D: *Memphis, Tennessee, September 18, 1966* | D: *Unknown* | D: *Unknown* | D: *Unknown* |

The Memphis Jug Band was organized by singer–guitarist Will Shade, also known as Son Brimmer, who was born in 1898 and spent most of his life in Memphis. Other members of the band included local musicians Ben Ramey, Charles Polk, and Will Weldon. Between 1927 and 1934 the group recorded nearly seventy-five sides, many of them infectiously up-tempo pieces. Their "Bottle It Up and Go" of 1932 became a blues standard of that decade.

**MEMPHIS JUG BAND**

# BIG BILL BROONZY

*B: Scott, Mississippi, June 26, 1893*
*D: Chicago, Illinois, August 15, 1958*

Born in 1893, William Lee Conley Broonzy — Big Bill
Broonzy — played violin in the vicinity of Little Rock,
Arkansas, before moving to Chicago, where he took up
guitar in the early 1920s. He first recorded in 1927
and became a hit-maker during the next decade,
enjoying a continuous recording career up to his death
in 1958. He was associated with a sound rather than a
signature song — his warm voice, facile touch, and
strong beat earned him popularity as both a city and
country blues stylist.

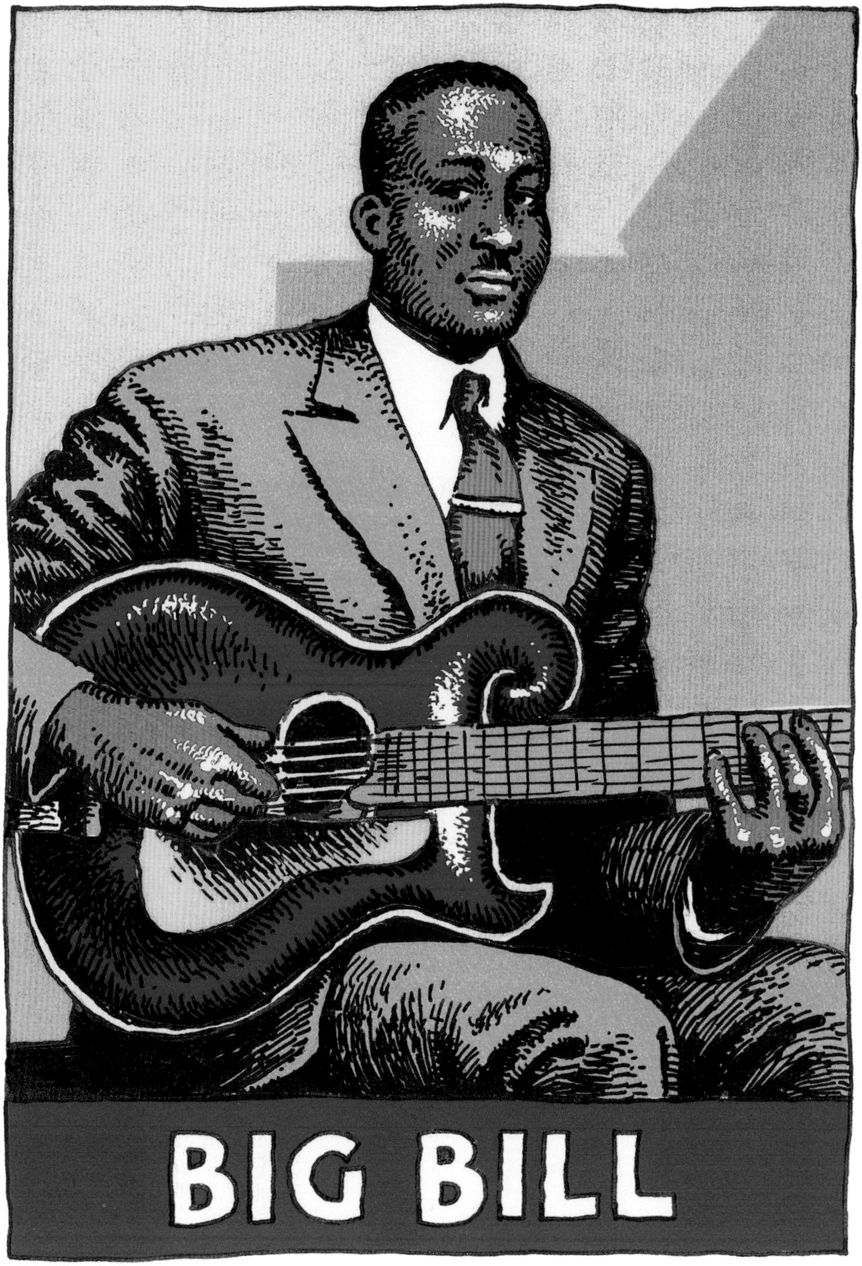
BIG BILL

# ROOSEVELT SYKES

B: *Helena, Arkansas, January 31, 1906*
D: *New Orleans, Louisiana, July 17, 1983*

Roosevelt Sykes, known as the Honeydripper, was born in 1906 and learned piano around 1918 in Helena, Arkansas. His main influence was Lee Green, from whom he derived his 1929 hit, "44 Blues." He began his recording career while living in St. Louis and produced nearly 125 sides between 1929 and 1942, some under the pseudonyms Willie Kelly and Dobby Boggs. Sykes continued as a postwar attraction and his career was enhanced during the 1960s blues revival.

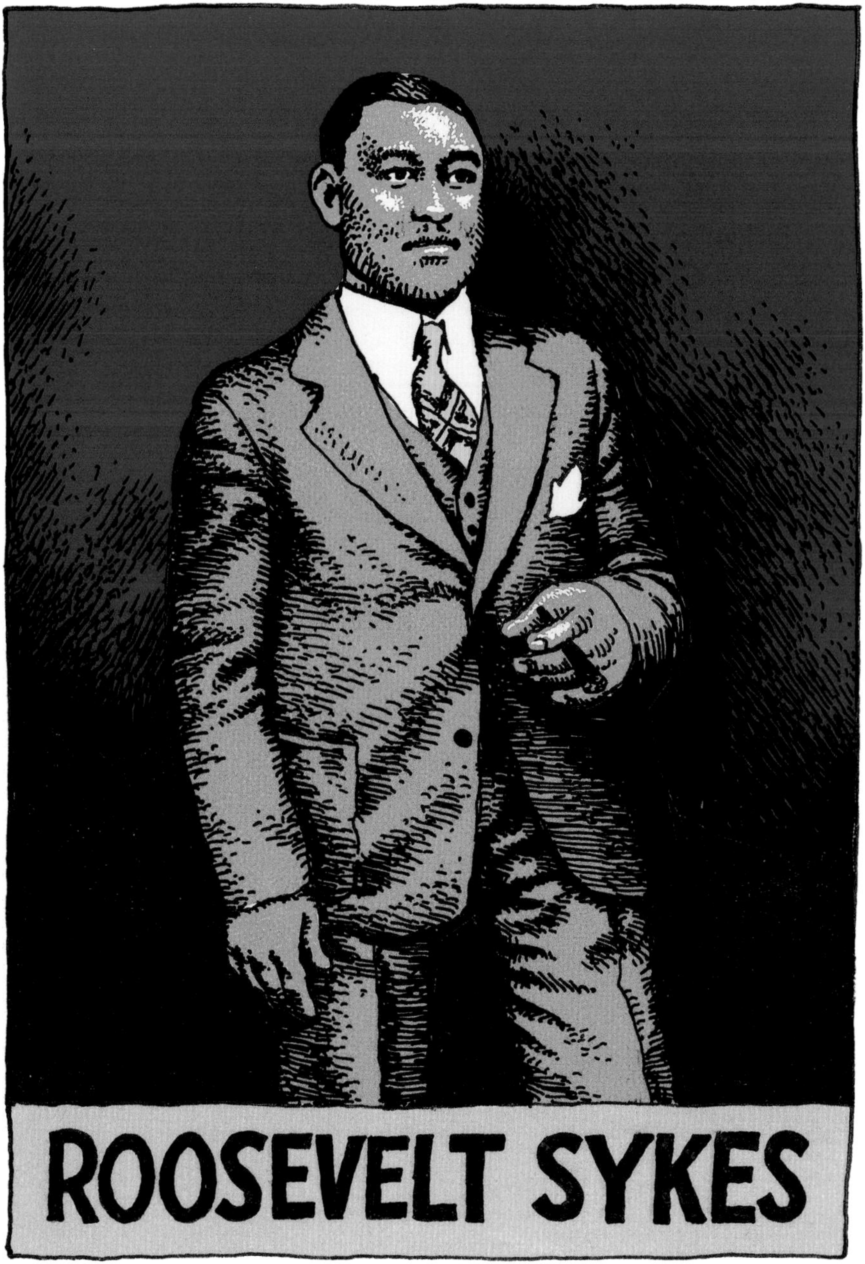

ROOSEVELT SYKES

# BLIND GARY DAVIS

*B: Laurens, South Carolina, April 30, 1896*
*D: Hammonton, New Jersey, May 5, 1972*

A native of Laurens, South Carolina, Gary Davis
learned to play the guitar around 1903, at the age of
seven. As a street singer, he specialized in gospel songs.
When he first recorded in 1935, he lived in Durham,
North Carolina, and counted the popular Blind Boy
Fuller as a protégé. Davis's magnificent guitar playing
earned him an avid following among northern audiences after he moved to New York in the 1940s, and
he toured and made numerous records before his
death in 1972.

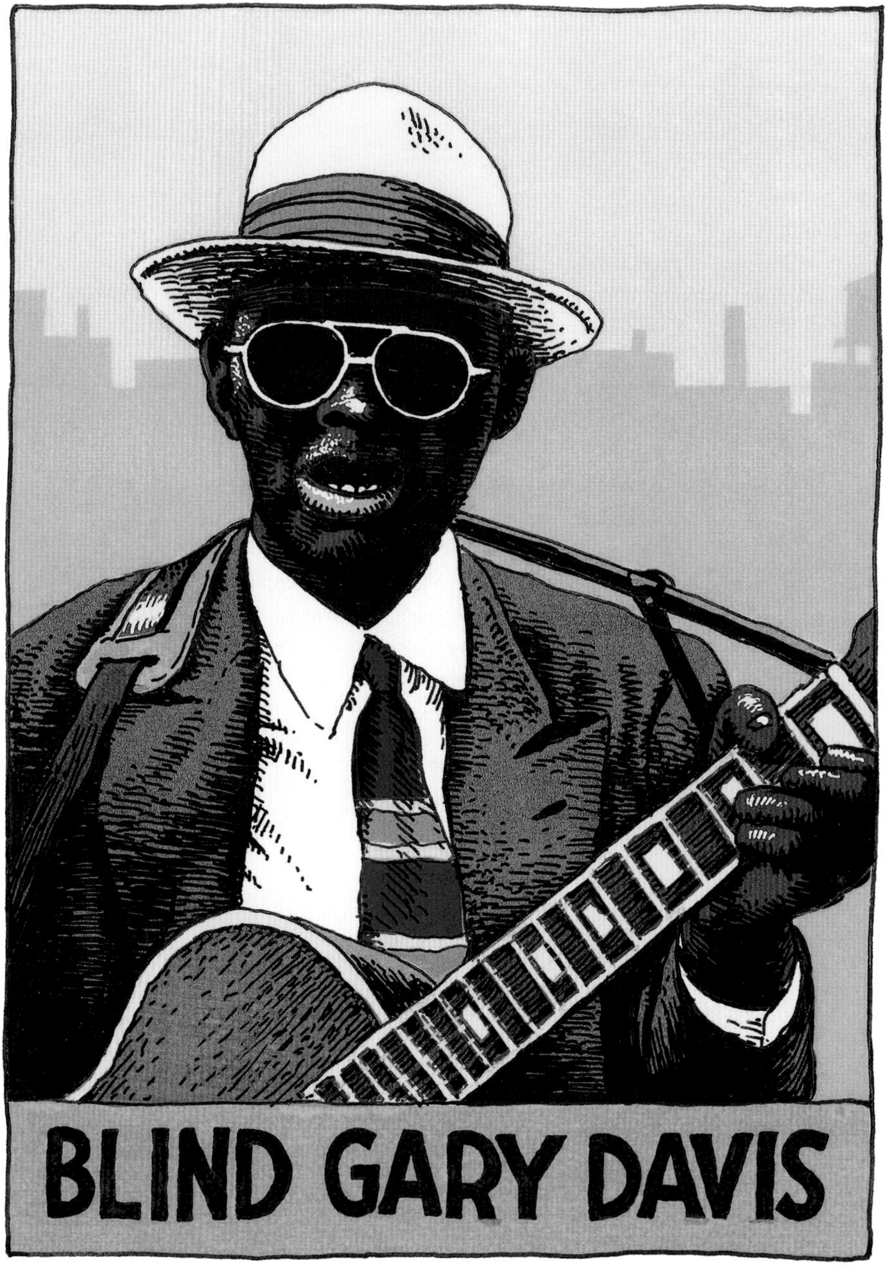
BLIND GARY DAVIS

# PAPA CHARLIE JACKSON

*B: New Orleans, Louisiana, 1885*
*D: Chicago, Illinois, 1938*

New Orleans musician Papa Charlie Jackson was one of
the first self-accompanied blues performers to record.
Discovered on the streets of Chicago, he produced
more than seventy sides between 1924 and 1935, most
of them on six-string banjo. Jackson combined sophisticated technique with a driving beat. His dance hit
"Shake That Thing" was one of the most influential
tunes of the era, and his comedic approach inspired the
hokum style of Georgia Tom and Tampa Red.

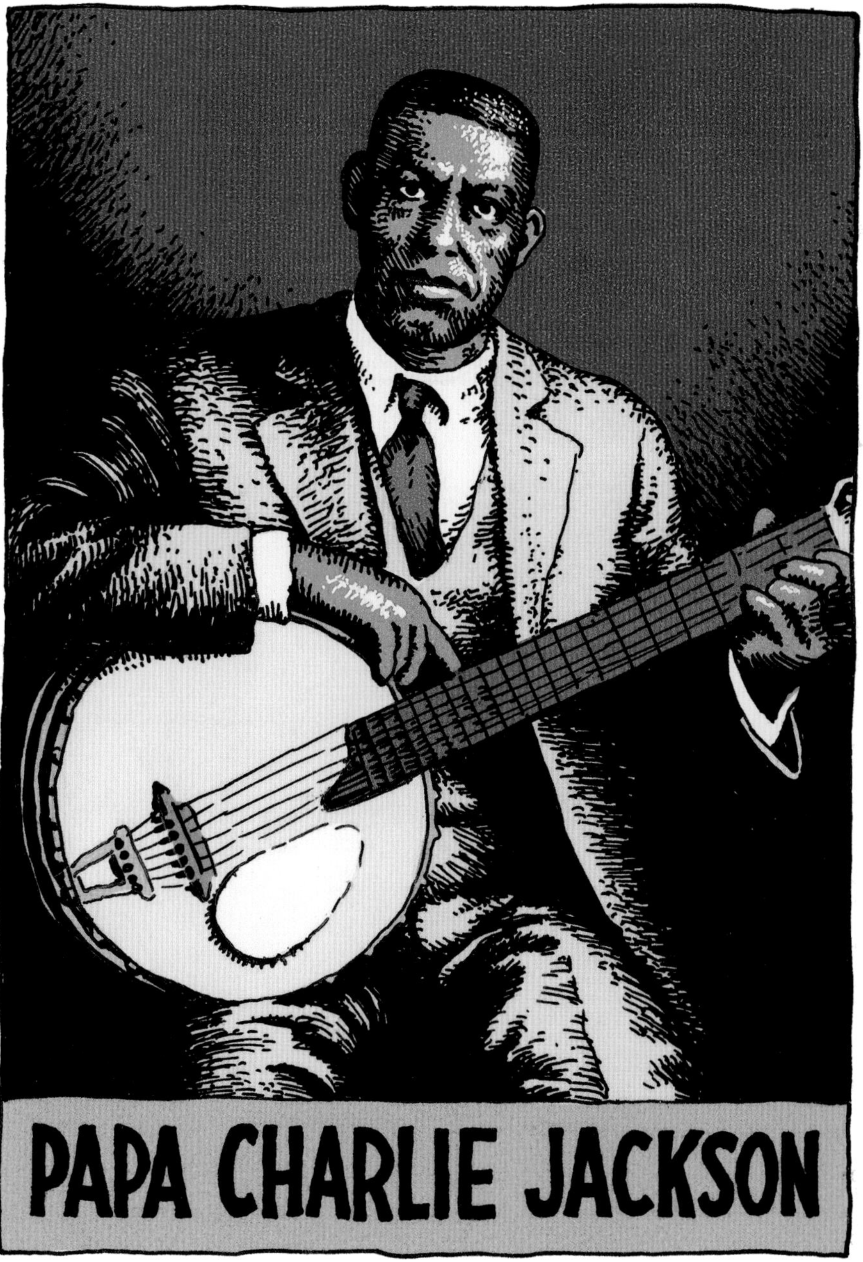

PAPA CHARLIE JACKSON

# CHARLEY PATTON

*B: Edwards, Mississippi, 1887*
*D: Indianola, Mississippi, April 28, 1934*

One of the most influential Mississippi blues musicians, Charley Patton was born in 1887 and raised in the Delta town of Dockery. By 1910 he was already an established performer, known for such songs as "Pony Blues." A prolific artist, he recorded more titles (forty-two) within a single year than any blues artist of the decade. After his debut in 1929, his blend of comedic effects and hard blues gave him a unique musical identity.

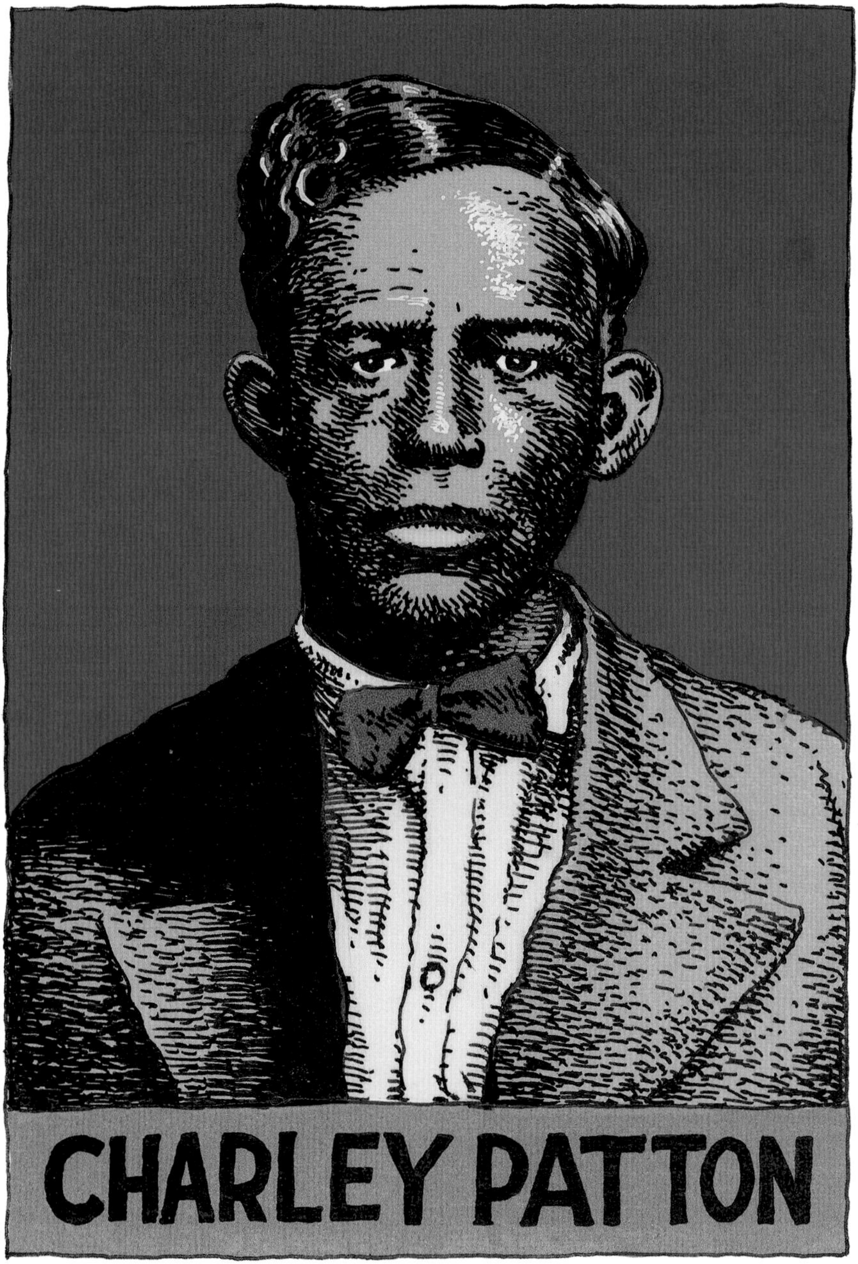

CHARLEY PATTON

# BUDDY BOY HAWKINS

Walter "Buddy Boy" Hawkins, reputedly a resident
of Blytheville, Arkansas, recorded twelve sides for
Paramount Records in 1927 and 1929. Details of his life
are scanty. Hawkins played exclusively in open A tuning
and utilized a sophisticated guitar style. His repertoire
included both fast, raggy songs and slow blues. His
timing and touch were impeccable, and his harmonies
were considerably more developed than those of
his peers, yet his records sold poorly and he faded
into obscurity.

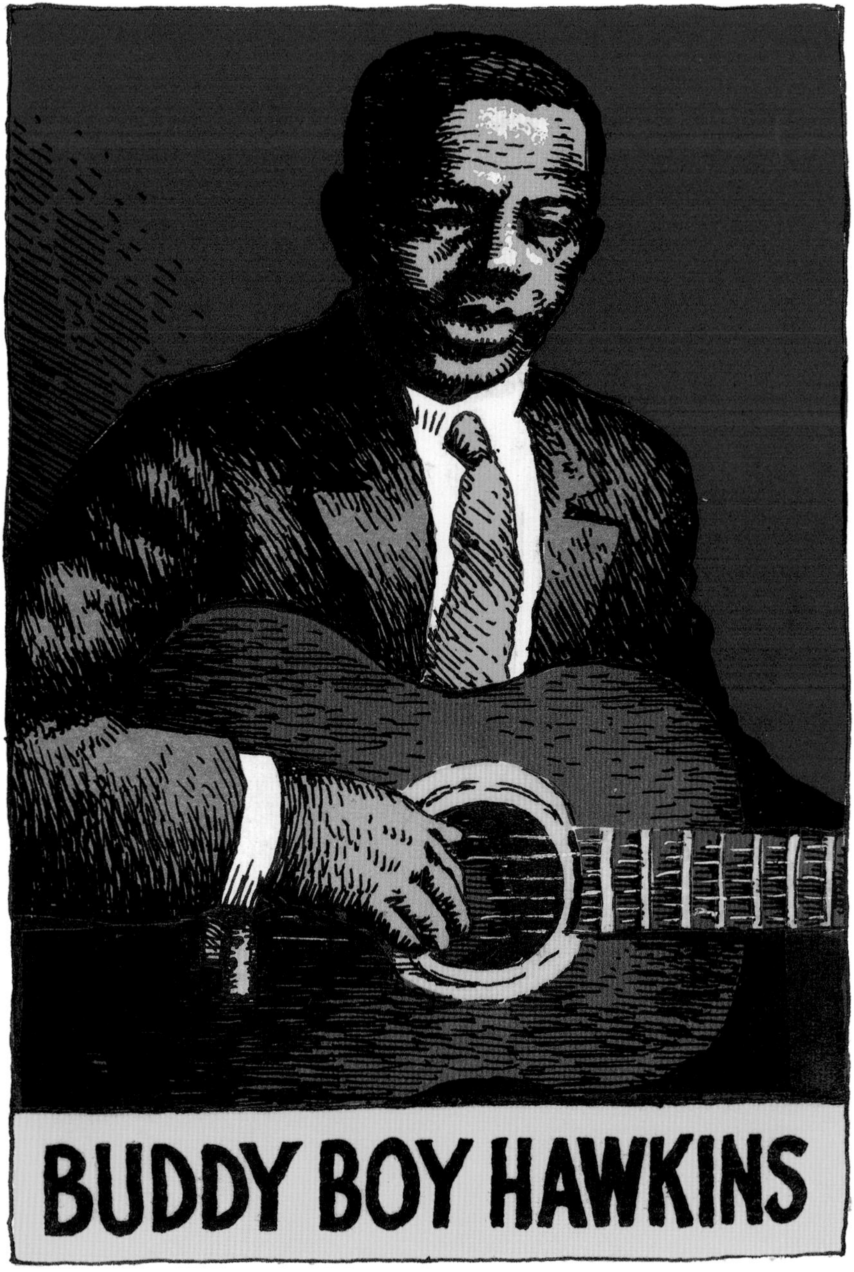

BUDDY BOY HAWKINS

# BARBECUE BOB

B: *Walnut Grove, Georgia, September 11, 1902*
D: *Lithonia, Georgia, October 21, 1931*

Robert Hicks was born in 1902 at Walnut Grove, Georgia, and learned guitar from his brother, who recorded under the name Charlie Lincoln. Around 1920 Hicks moved to Atlanta; his employment at a local restaurant gave rise to his recording name, Barbecue Bob. Between 1927 and 1930 Hicks recorded fifty-five sides. His twelve-string guitar style was among the most percussive found in blues, setting him apart from some like-sounding Georgians.

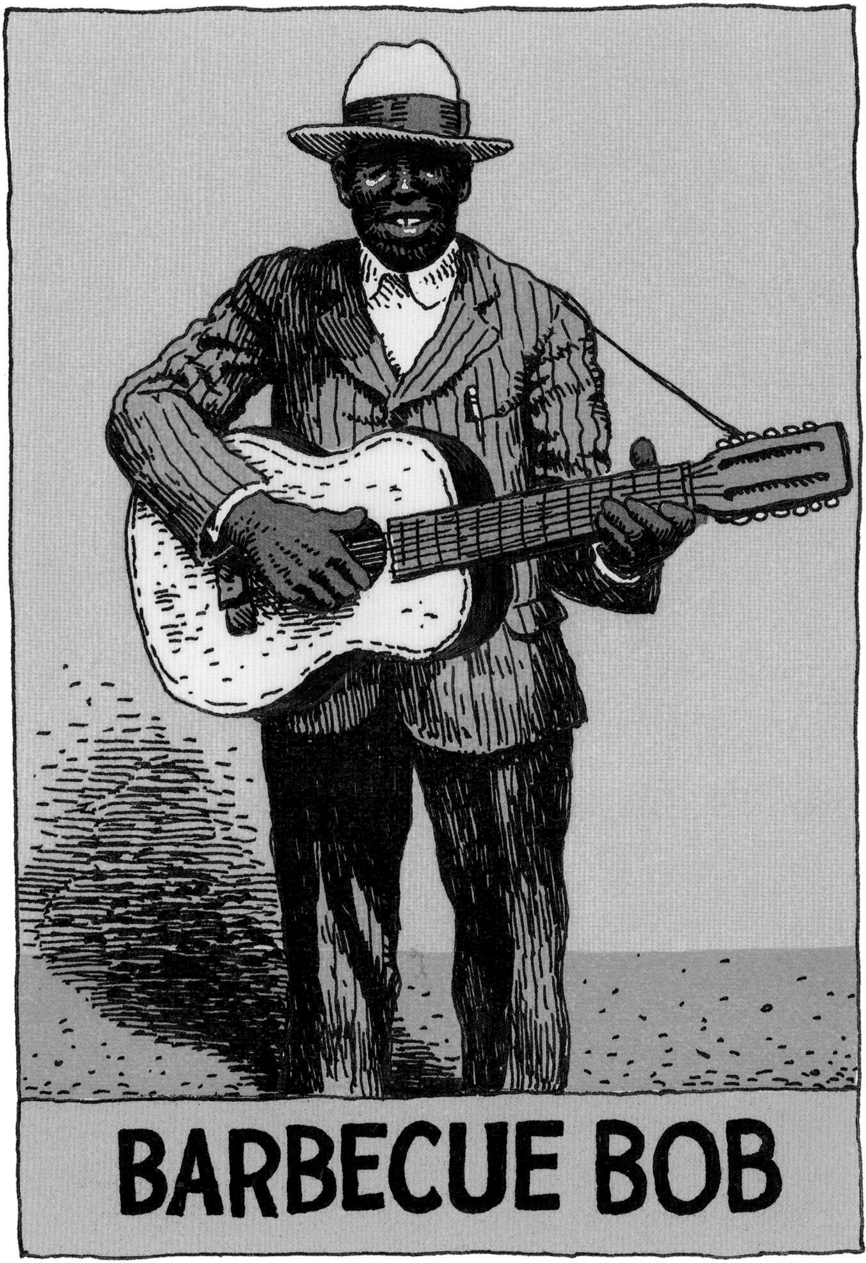

BARBECUE BOB

# ED BELL

*B: Forest Deposit, Alabama, May 1905*
*D: Greenville, Alabama, 1960*

Ed Bell was born around 1905 and raised in Greenville, Alabama. He is said to have derived his style from an older Alabamian, Joe Pat Dean. Bell first recorded in 1927 and, in addition to the music released under his own name, he also used the pseudonyms Sluefoot Joe (with Clifford Gibson) and Barefoot Bill. Taken together, the blues recorded under these three names form a unique style. Bell gave up music for the pulpit during the Depression.

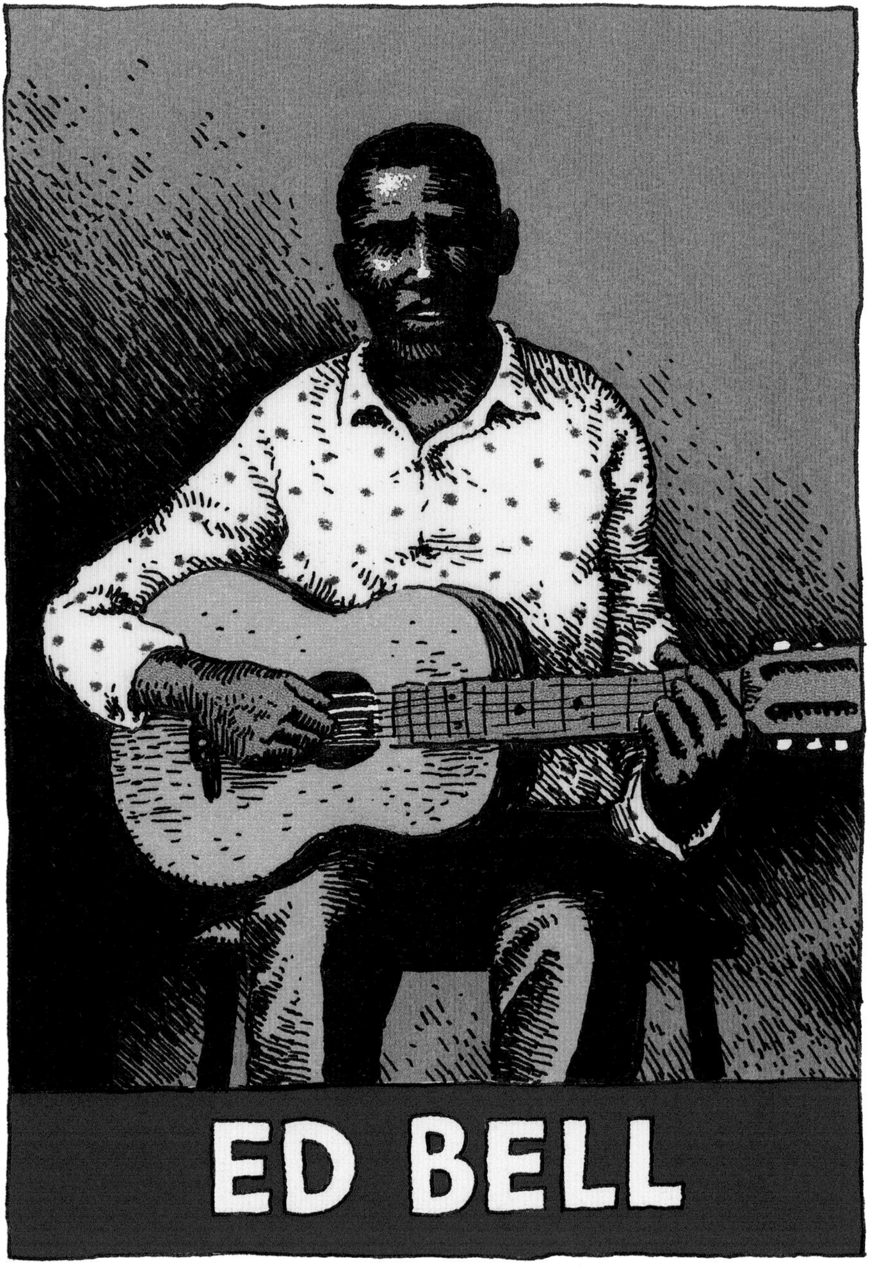
ED BELL

# BLIND WILLIE McTELL

*B: Thompson, Georgia, May 5, 1901*
*D: Milledgeville, Georgia, August 19, 1959*

Born in Thompson, Georgia, in 1901, Willie McTell learned guitar from his mother around 1914 and made his recording debut in 1927 after working as a street singer and medicine-show minstrel. Over the next nine years he recorded forty-eight sides for four companies under four different names, sometimes teamed with his wife, Kate McTell. A deft guitarist with a sweet voice, McTell made Library of Congress blues field recordings and postwar records for the R & B market as well.

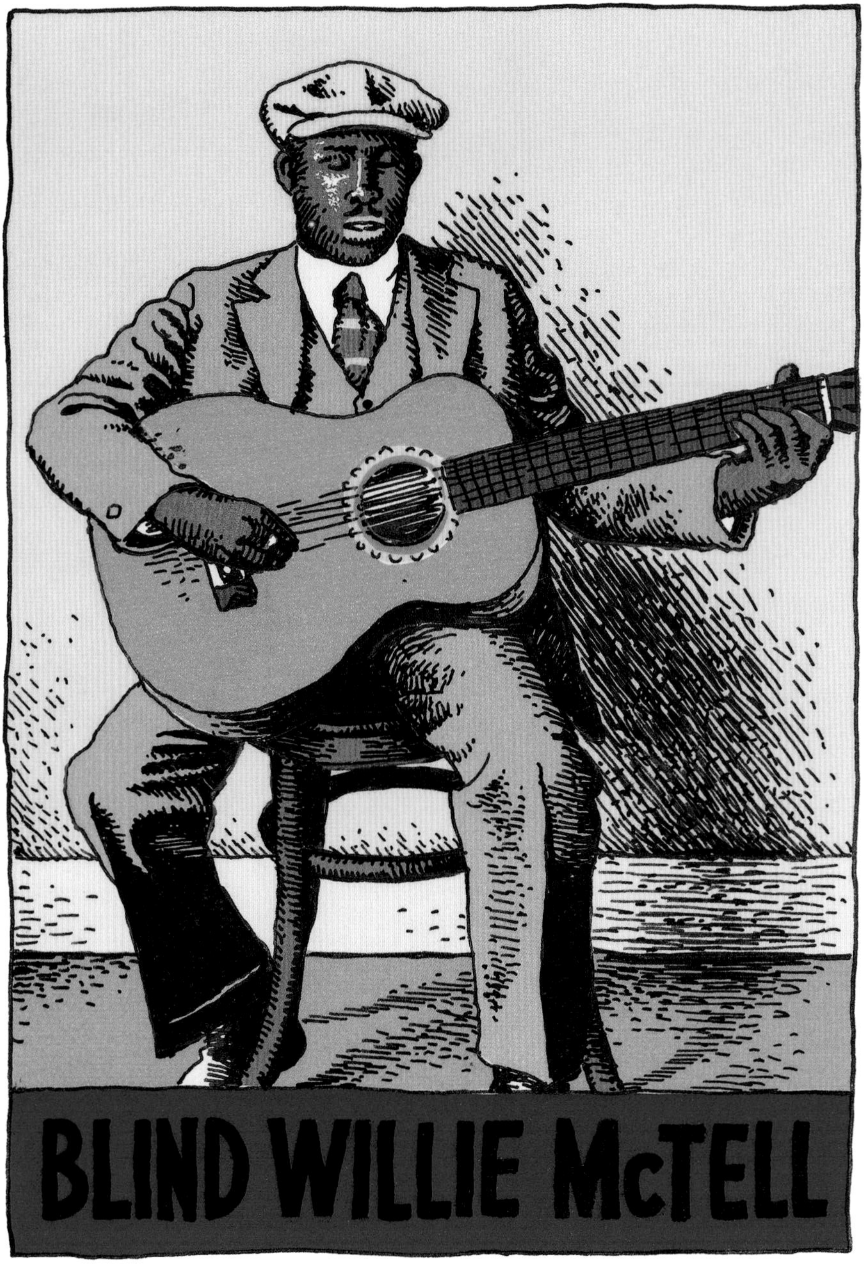
BLIND WILLIE McTELL

# SON HOUSE

*B: Riverton, Mississippi, March 21, 1902*
*D: Detroit, Michigan, October 19, 1988*

The possessor of a powerful voice, Eddie James "Son" House gave up preaching for music around 1927 while in his native Lyon, Mississippi. His friend Charley Patton arranged for his 1930 recording debut, which resulted in nine titles. He worked with Willie Brown and recorded for the Library of Congress before moving to Rochester, New York, in 1943. House influenced such famed musicians as Robert Johnson and Muddy Waters. His career revived when he was rediscovered in 1964.

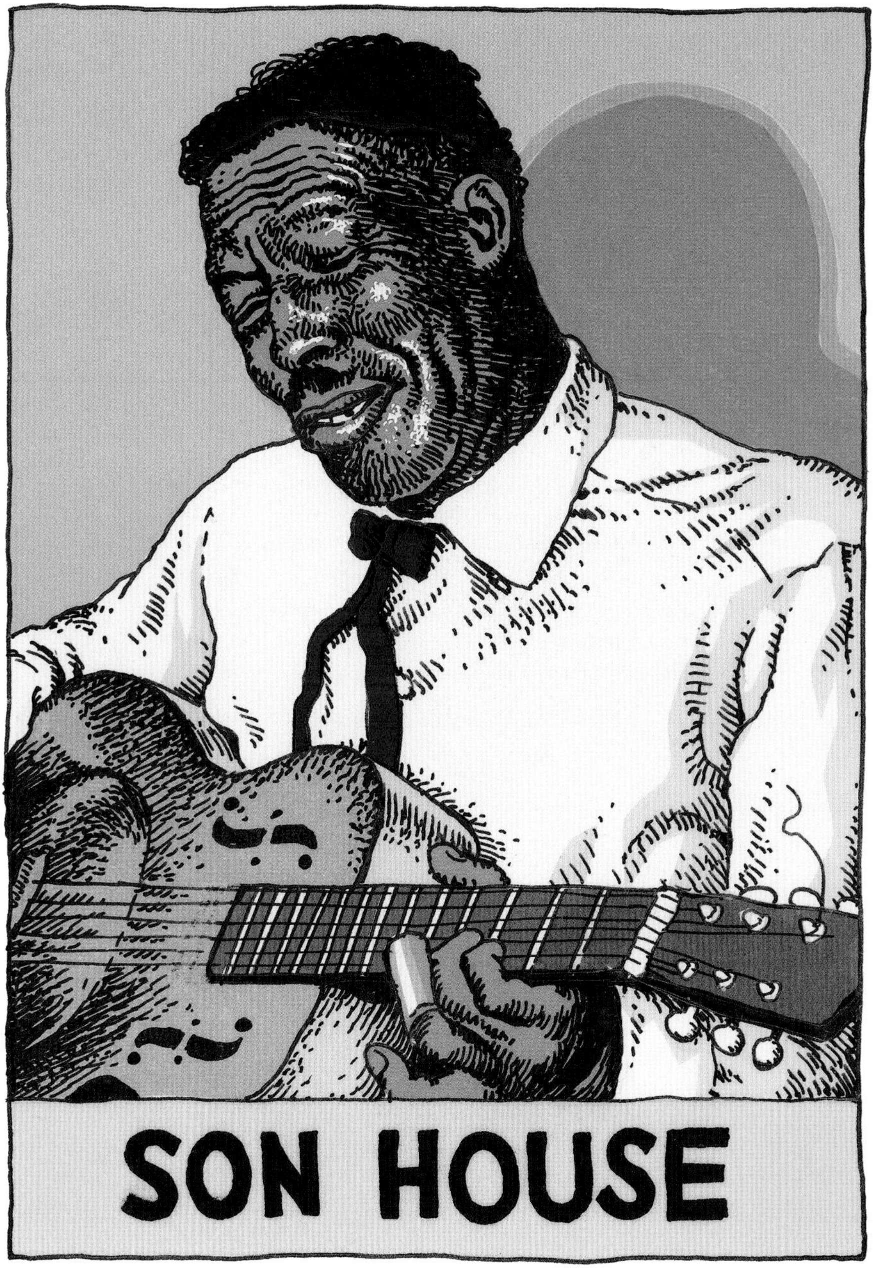

SON HOUSE

# MEMPHIS MINNIE

*B: Algiers, Louisiana, June 3, 1897*
*D: Memphis, Tennessee, August 6, 1973*

Lizzie Douglas, born in Algiers, Louisiana, was raised
in Memphis, and learned guitar at the age of eleven. As
Kid Douglas, she toured the South from 1916 onward,
returning to Memphis in the late 1920s under the name
Memphis Minnie. An accomplished guitarist and gifted
songwriter, she recorded more than 150 sides between
1929 and 1941. Most were solo blues, but she also
teamed for duets with her second husband, guitarist
Kansas Joe McCoy, and her third husband, guitarist
Little Son Joe Lawlar.

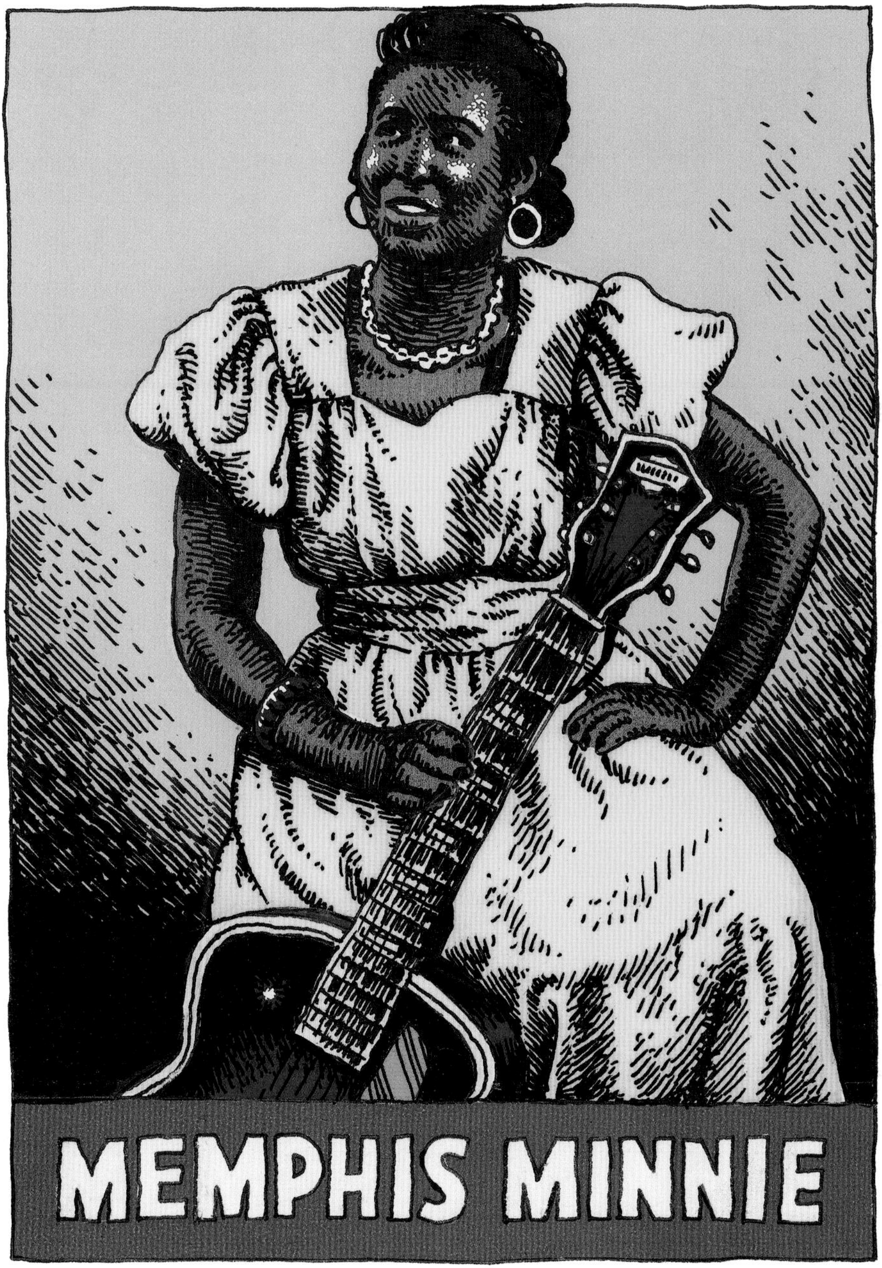

MEMPHIS MINNIE

# MISSISSIPPI JOHN HURT

B: *Teoc, Carroll County, Mississippi, March 8, 1892 (or July 3, 1893)*
D: *Grenada, Mississippi, November 2, 1966*

John Hurt was born in 1892 or 1893 (sources vary) at Teoc, Carroll County, Mississippi, and raised in nearby Avalon. He took up guitar in 1903, developing a soft singing style and a unique three-finger picking technique. Never a professional musician, Hurt rarely traveled before or after recording twelve sides for Okeh Records in 1928, but his 1960s rediscovery helped launch a blues revival, and he performed and re-recorded songs such as "Coffee Blues" and "Richland Woman" to great acclaim before his death in 1966.

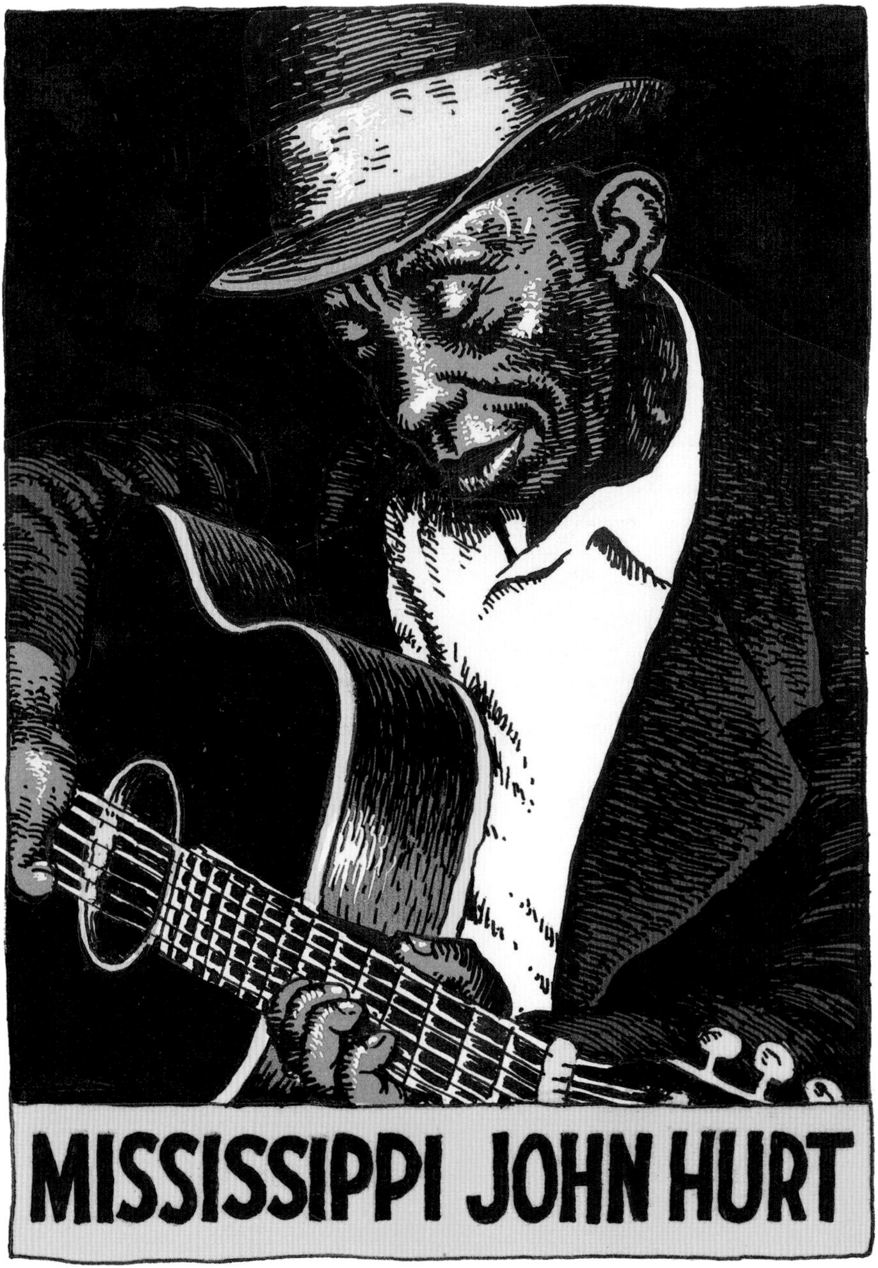
MISSISSIPPI JOHN HURT

# TOMMY JOHNSON

B: *Near Terry, Mississippi, c. 1896*
D: *Crystal Springs, Mississippi, November 1, 1956*

An outstanding vocalist whose trademark falsetto was widely copied, Tommy Johnson was born around 1896 near Terry, Mississippi. He took up music around 1914 and was influenced by Delta performer Charley Patton, although his guitar playing was far more ragged than his mentor's. Johnson's travels made him a familiar figure throughout the Mississippi Delta. Between 1928 and 1930 he recorded eleven sides, including the popular "Big Road Blues."

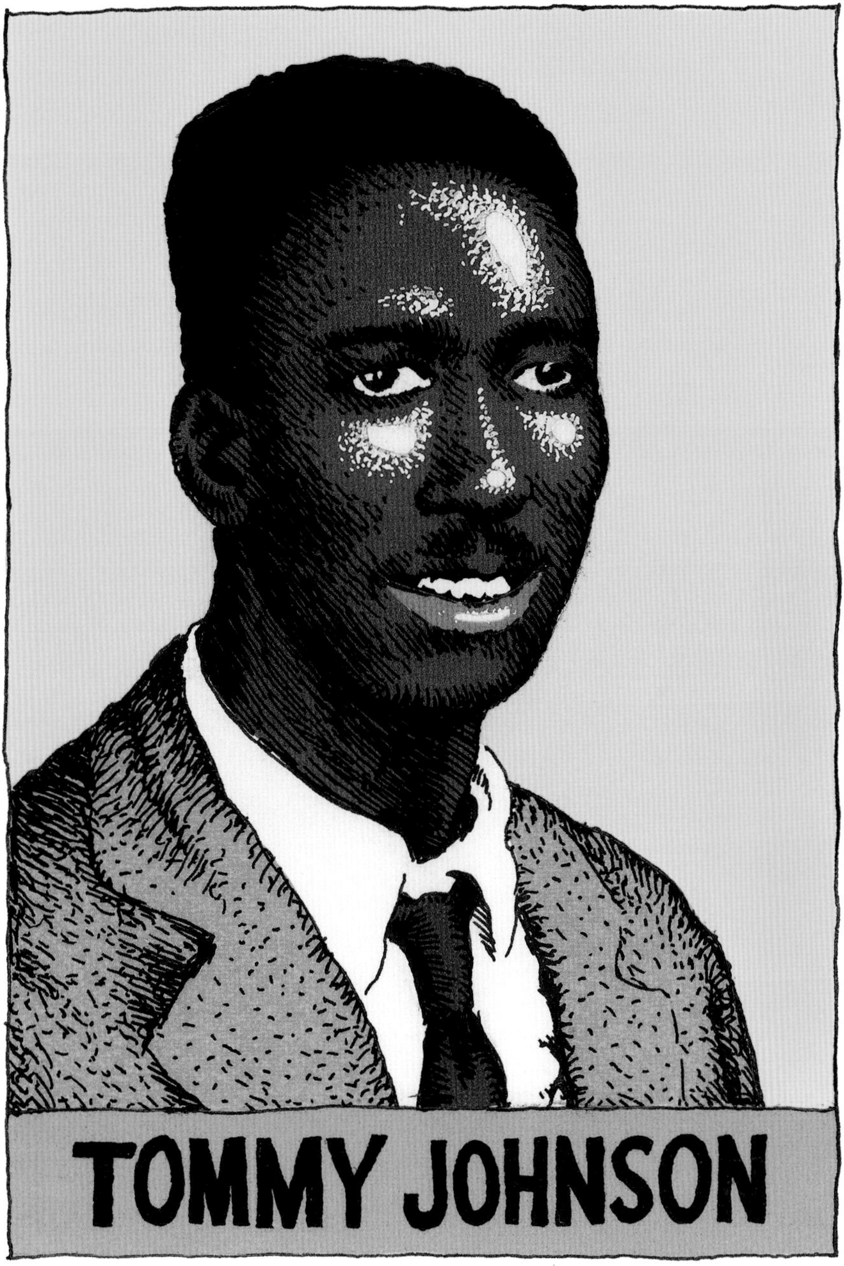

TOMMY JOHNSON

# PEETIE WHEATSTRAW

*B: Ripley, Tennessee, December 21, 1902*
*D: East St. Louis, Illinois, December 21, 1941*

Peetie Wheatstraw was born William Bunch at Ripley,
Tennessee, in 1902. He lived for a time in Cotton Plant,
Arkansas, then moved north in 1929. Working largely
out of St. Louis, he became one of the blues' most popular vocalists, and recorded 161 titles between 1930
and 1941. His style of interjecting a fleeting falsetto on
the last measure of a verse was the most widely copied
blues mannerism of the period. A fatal car accident
cut short his career in 1941.

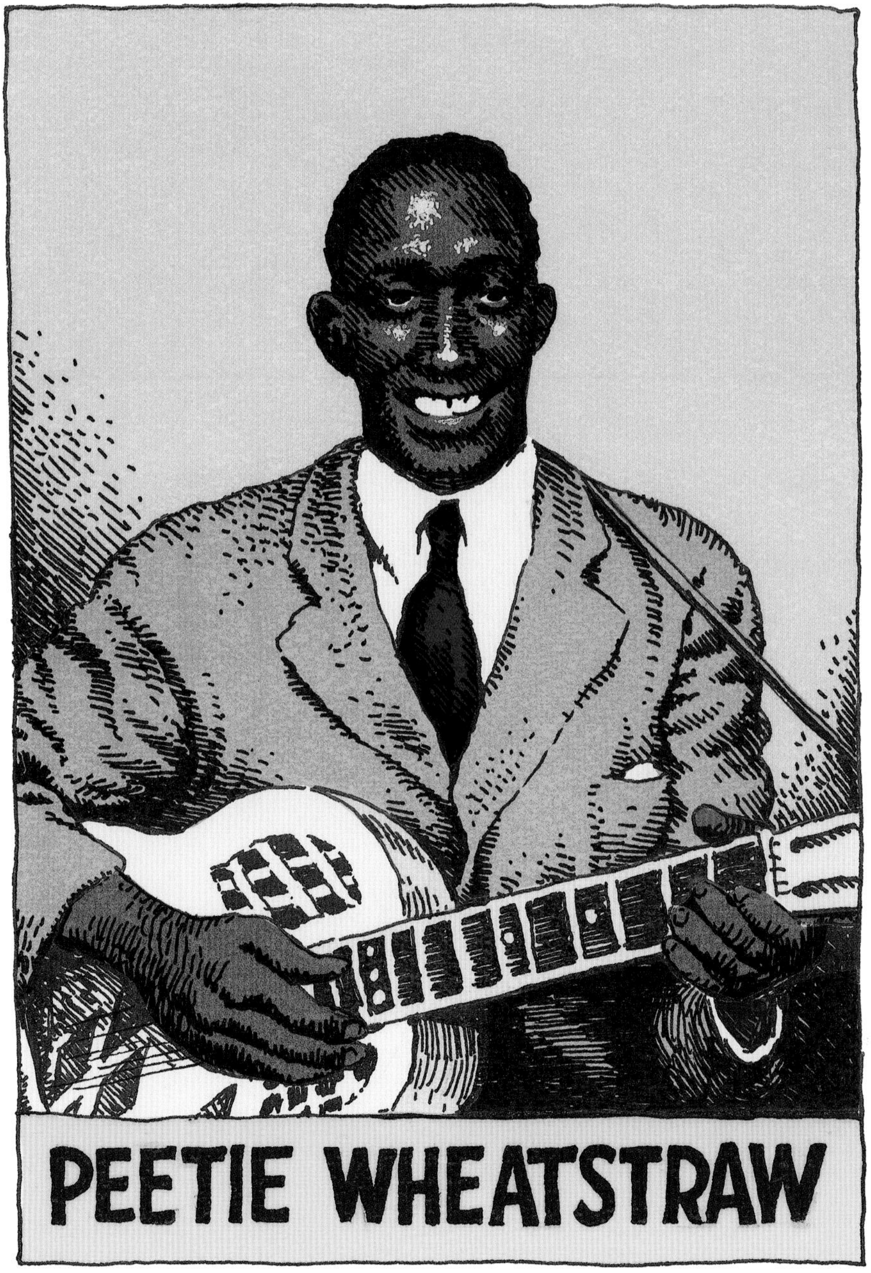

PEETIE WHEATSTRAW

# BO CARTER

*B: Bolton, Mississippi, March 21, 1893*
*D: Memphis, Tennessee, September 21, 1964*

Armenter Chatmon, better known as Bo Carter, was
raised in Bolton, Mississippi. He learned guitar in the
early 1900s, played double bass in a family string band
led by his brother, Lonnie Chatmon, in the 1910s,
and later joined the Mississippi Sheiks (see page 38).
Carter's career as a street singer was largely imposed
by the blindness that afflicted him in the late 1920s.
Between 1930 and 1940 he recorded 105 titles, many
notable for their musical sophistication and for the
clever sexual innuendo of their lyrics.

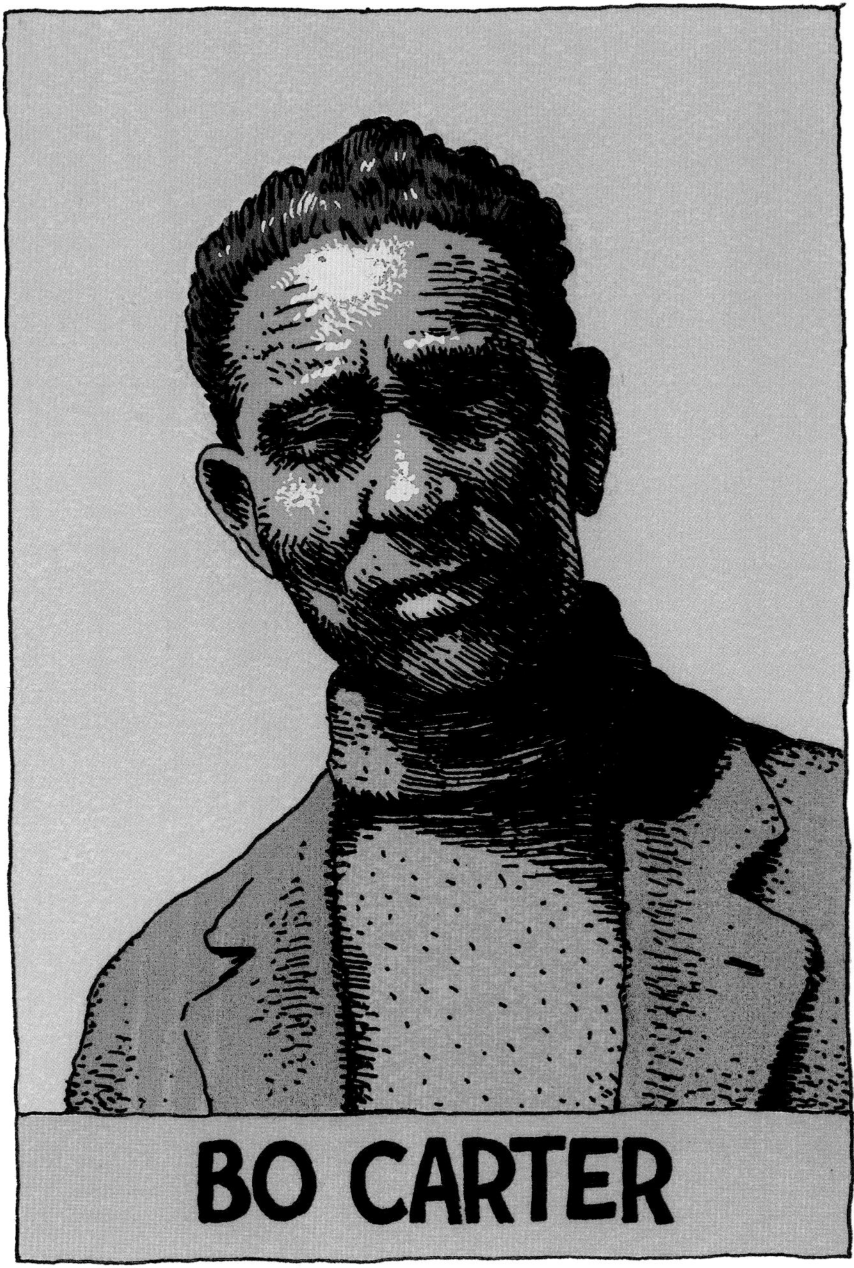

BO CARTER

# "BIX" BEIDERBECKE

**CORNET**

*B: Davenport, Iowa, March 10, 1903*
*D: New York, New York, August 6, 1931*

"Bix" Beiderbecke was one of the most influential cornetists in early jazz history. His tone, characterized by perfect pitch and spare, well-placed notes, was clean and bell-like. He came to prominence while with Dick Voynow's Wolverines, which made a series of historic recordings for Gennett Records in 1924. His next important engagement was with Jean Goldkette's Orchestra in 1926, followed in late 1927 by Paul Whiteman's large orchestra. Among the most important recordings ever made were the ones under the name Bix and His Gang from October 1927 to September 1928 for Okeh Records.

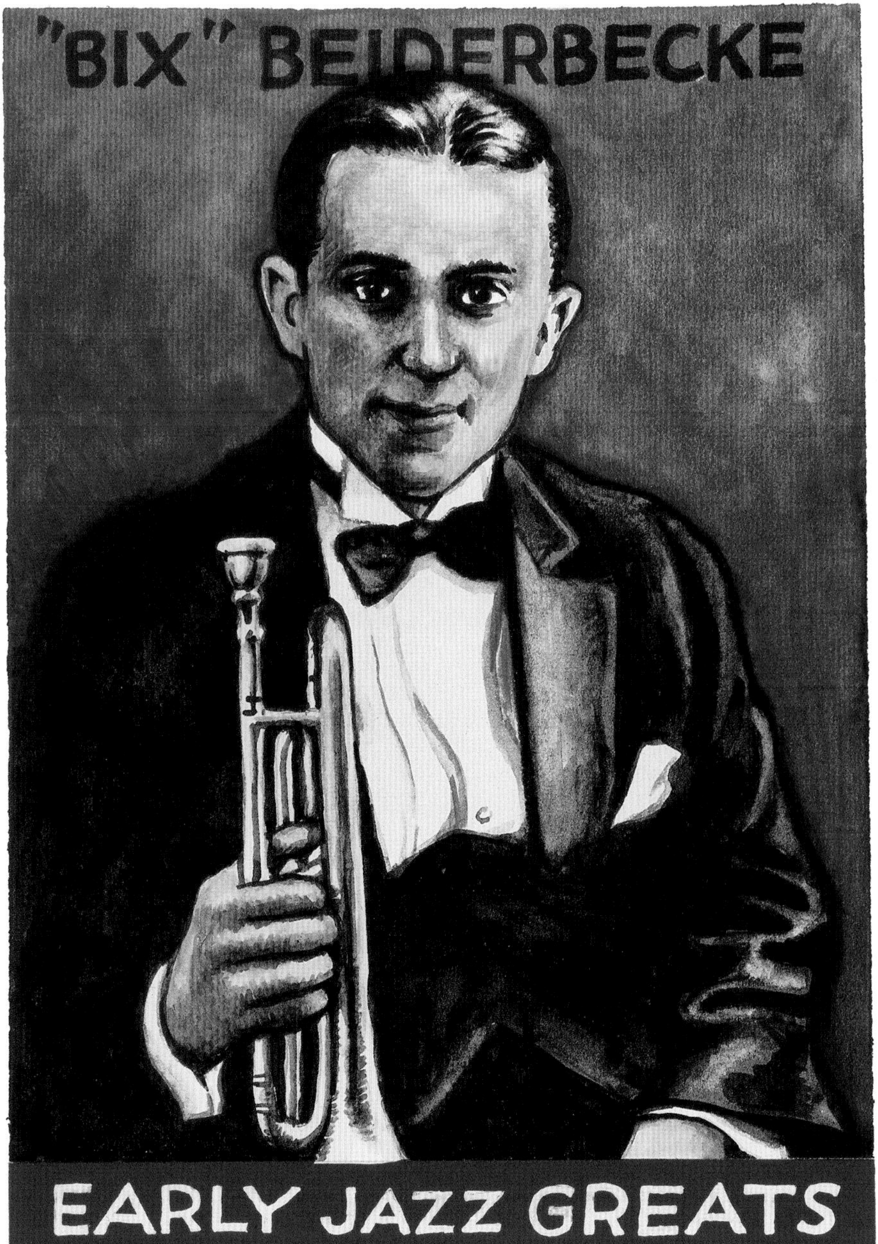
"BIX" BEIDERBECKE
EARLY JAZZ GREATS

# COLEMAN HAWKINS

**TENOR SAXOPHONE, CLARINET, BASS SAXOPHONE**

*B: St. Joseph, Missouri, November 21, 1904*
*D: New York, New York, May 19, 1969*

Coleman Hawkins, the first great tenor saxophonist in jazz, was playing in a Kansas City pit band when Mamie Smith signed him to her Jazz Hounds in 1921. In 1924 he joined Fletcher Henderson's Orchestra, having recorded with that group a year earlier on clarinet and bass saxophone. He toured Europe as a soloist and freelancer from 1934 to 1939, led his own U.S.–based band in the 1940s, and thereafter freelanced in Europe and America. Hawkins played at every major jazz festival in the world, appeared in films, and made thousands of records, the most famous of which is "Body and Soul," recorded with his own band for Bluebird in 1939.

COLEMAN
HAWKINS

EARLY JAZZ GREATS

# "JELLY ROLL" MORTON

**PIANO, ARRANGER**
B: *Gulfport, Louisiana, September 20, 1885*
D: *Los Angeles, California, July 10, 1941*

Born Ferdinand Joseph La Menthe, "Jelly Roll" Morton grew up in New Orleans, where he played piano in the most prestigious sporting houses in Storyville. He was the earliest of the jazzmen who insisted upon a recognizable style of playing. His concept of trying to sound like a Dixieland jazz band on the piano was unique. His ideal jazz band came to life in a series of recordings his Red Hot Peppers made for RCA Victor Records in 1926. His genius is reflected in his compositions, all of which are jazz standards.

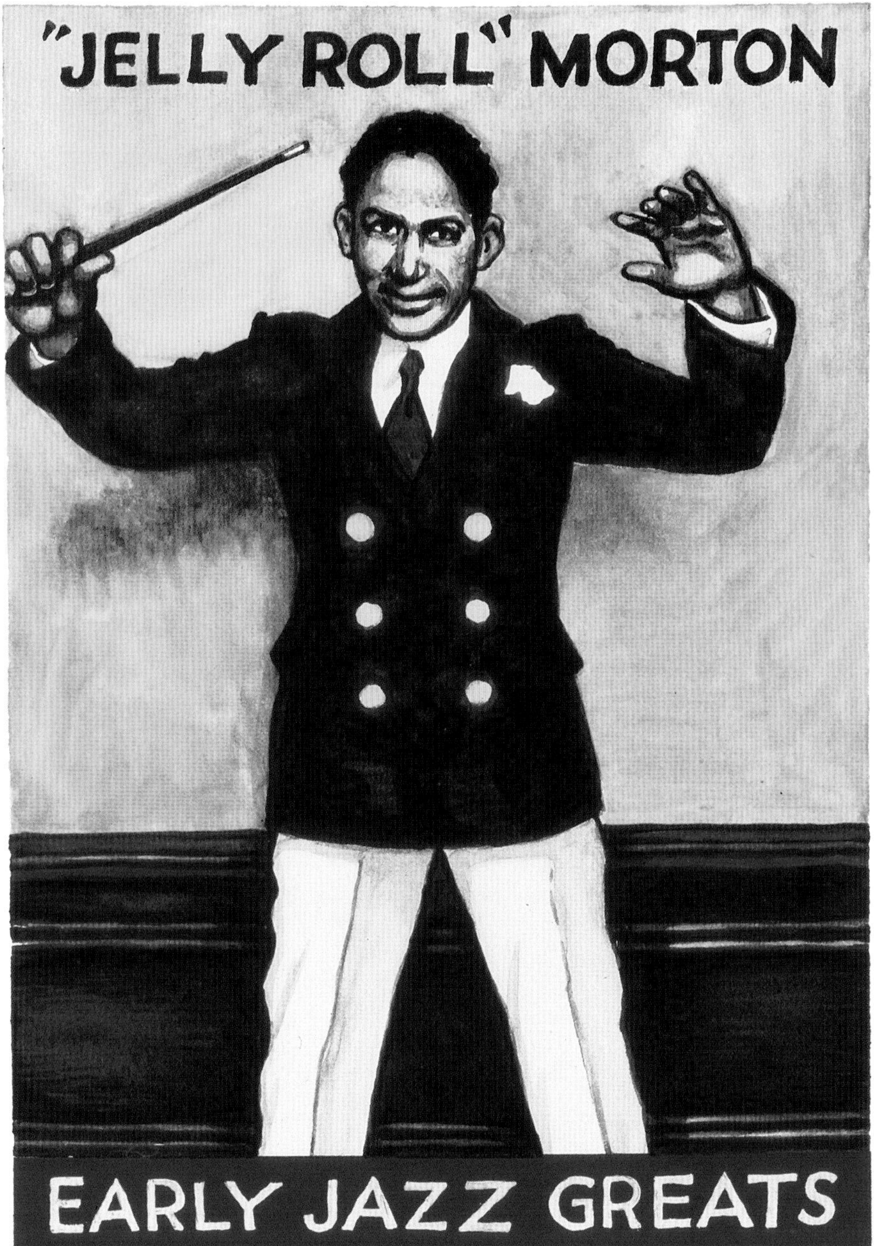
"JELLY ROLL" MORTON
EARLY JAZZ GREATS

# LOUIS ARMSTRONG

**TRUMPET, VOCALS**
B: *New Orleans, Louisiana, July 4, 1900*
D: *New York, New York, July 6, 1971*

The most imitated and among the most influential
trumpeters in jazz, Louis Armstrong started his career
under the tutelage of King Oliver. His first professional
job was with Fate Marable's Orchestra aboard the
Streckfus steamboats around New Orleans. Armstrong
joined King Oliver's Creole Jazz Band in Chicago in
1922, and made his first recordings with that group in the
following year. In 1924 he joined Fletcher Henderson's
band in New York. Armstrong moved back to Chicago
at the end of 1925 and made his first recordings with his
own band, the Hot Five. Illustrious colleagues included
Earl Hines and Erskine Tate, with whom he recorded
from 1926 to 1928. Throughout the 1930s he fronted
Luis Russell's band. In 1947, Armstrong formed his All
Stars which toured the world. He was America's official
Ambassador of Jazz.

LOUIS ARMSTRONG

EARLY JAZZ GREATS

# LIL HARDIN

**PIANO**

B: *Memphis, Tennessee, February 3, 1898*
D: *Chicago, Illinois, August 27, 1971*

Lillian "Lil" Hardin studied music at Fisk University.
In 1917 she moved to Chicago, where she began her
career as a song demonstrator. She played with Freddie
Keppard, led her own group in 1920, and was in King
Oliver's Creole Jazz Band from 1921 to 1924. In
February 1924 she married Louis Armstrong and formed
the Dreamland Syncopators, which Armstrong joined
in 1925. She in turn recorded with Armstrong's Hot
Five and Hot Seven bands. The couple divorced in 1938.
Hardin performed on NBC radio, was a Decca studio
pianist, led many bands, freelanced, and soloed around
the world until her death in 1971.

LIL HARDIN

EARLY JAZZ GREATS

# JOHNNY DODDS

**CLARINET, ALTO SAXOPHONE**
B: *New Orleans, Louisiana, April 12, 1892*
D: *Chicago, Illinois, August 8, 1940*

One of the greatest and most influential jazz clarinetists, Johnny Dodds began taking lessons when he was seventeen from the seminal stylist Lorenzo Tio, Jr. By 1911 Dodds was working in New Orleans with Kid Ory and Fate Marable. He moved to Chicago in 1922, joined King Oliver's Creole Jazz Band, and made many recordings with the jazz greats of his time, including King Oliver, Freddie Keppard, and "Jelly Roll" Morton. Dodds was a member of Louis Armstrong's Hot Five and Hot Seven and led his own band throughout the 1930s. His clarinet style is distinctive and noted for its low register and blues inflections.

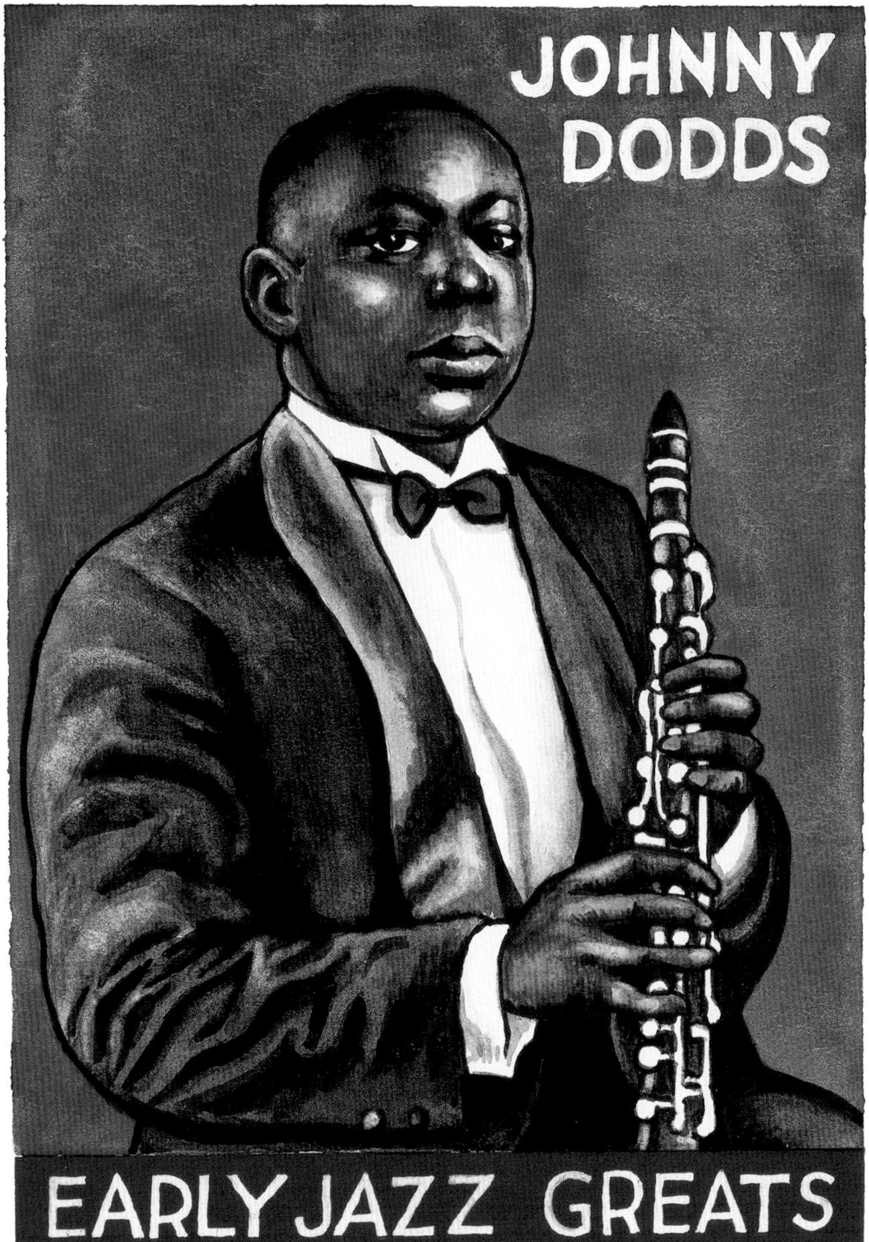
JOHNNY
DODDS
EARLY JAZZ GREATS

# EDDIE LANG

**GUITAR**

*B: Philadelphia, Pennsylvania, October 25, 1902*
*D: New York, New York, March 26, 1933*

Eddie Lang, born Salvatore Massaro, was classically trained on violin and guitar. Violinist Joe Venuti, his boyhood friend, was his musical partner — an association that lasted until Lang's premature death from complications of a tonsillectomy. After touring with the Mound City Blue Blowers, Lang began recording in 1925 at sessions featuring the likes of Venuti, "Bix" Beiderbecke, Frank Trumbauer, and Bing Crosby. Lang's 1928−29 duets with blues guitarist Lonnie Johnson are a high point in jazz history. The most recorded guitarist of the 1920s, Lang single-handedly made the banjo obsolete as a jazz instrument.

EDDIE
LANG

EARLY JAZZ GREATS

# JUNIE C. COBB

**SAXOPHONE**
*B: Hot Springs, Arkansas, 1896*
*D: Chicago, Illinois, January 1, 1970*

Junius "Junie" C. Cobb joined King Oliver's popular
and influential Creole Jazz Band on banjo in late 1924
and then in 1928 went off with Jimmy Noone. Cobb
formed his own band and toured Europe in 1950, playing saxophone and clarinet. Returning to Chicago after
his tour, he played clubs with his own band. In 1946
he began a new career as a solo pianist, which lasted
until his retirement from music in 1955.

JUNIE C. COBB

EARLY JAZZ GREATS

# JOE "KING" OLIVER

**CORNET**
B: *Abend, Louisiana, May 11, 1885*
D: *Savannah, Georgia, April 8, 1938*

Without doubt, Joe "King" Oliver was the first important jazz cornetist. Raised in Louisiana, he played in bands in New Orleans through the teens before forming his Creole Jazz Band in Chicago at Lincoln Gardens in June 1922, which made history with their Gennett Records recordings of April 1923. Of the many who learned from the King, it was Louis Armstrong who benefited the most from his tutelage. Oliver's big band of 1926–28, the Dixie Syncopators, consisted of a who's who in black jazz of the time. He further contributed several compositions that have become a standard part of the jazz repertoire, including "Dippermouth Blues," "Canal Street Blues," and "Doctor Jazz."

JOE "KING" OLIVER

EARLY JAZZ GREATS

# IKEY ROBINSON

**BANJO, GUITAR**

B: *Dublin, Virginia, July 28, 1904*
D: *Chicago, Illinois, October 25, 1990*

Ikey Robinson started his career as a banjo player locally in 1922. After moving to Chicago in 1926, he worked with "Jelly Roll" Morton's group, the Alabamians, and Sammy Stewart's band. Robinson went to New York in 1930, where he worked for Wilbur Sweatman and Noble Sissie. He recorded with Clarence Williams, Jabbo Smith, and under his own name from 1929 to 1935. Throughout the 1960s, he was with Franz Jackson's Original Jazz All-Stars. Robinson was noted for his intricate and melodically complex single-string picking.

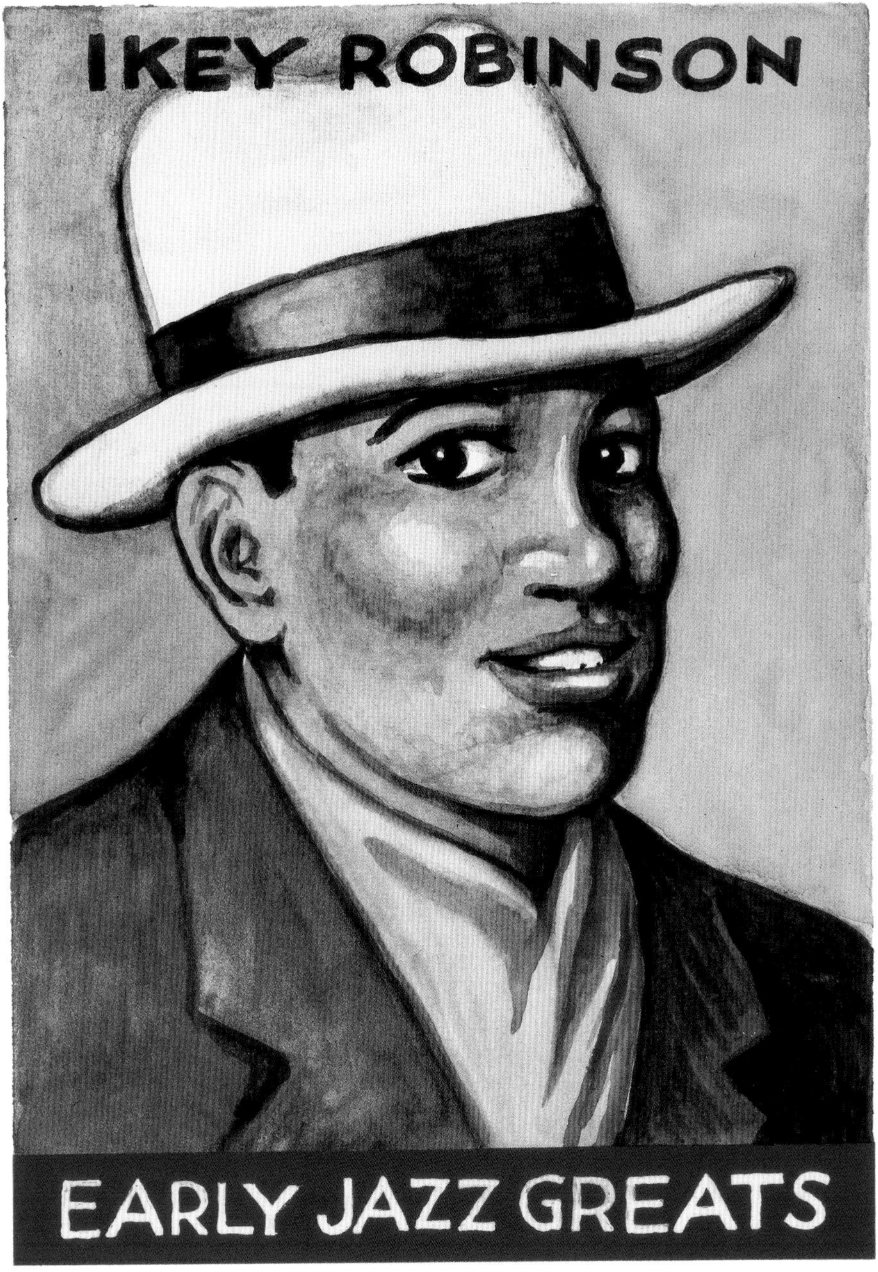
IKEY ROBINSON
EARLY JAZZ GREATS

# ROY PALMER

**TROMBONE**

*B: New Orleans, Louisiana, 1892*
*D: Chicago, Illinois, January 1964*

Roy Palmer began as a trombonist in Richard M. Jones's
band in 1911 in New Orleans. Moving to Chicago in
1917, he joined Lawrence Duhe in Sugar Johnny Smith's
Band. Throughout the 1920s he played in many local
Chicago bands. His pupils included Albert Wynn and
Preston Jackson, both of whom are well represented on
recordings. Palmer recorded with "Jelly Roll" Morton,
Jimmy Blythe, the Memphis Nighthawks, the Chicago
Rhythm Kings, Richard M. Jones and His Jazz Wizards,
and Johnny Dodds's Black Bottom Stompers.

# ROY PALMER

## EARLY JAZZ GREATS

# JACK TEAGARDEN

**TROMBONE**
B: *Vernon, Texas, August 29, 1905*
D: *New Orleans, Louisiana, January 15, 1964*

Jack Teagarden learned trombone at the age of ten, and by fifteen he was playing in local bands. He joined Ben Pollack in New York in 1928 and recorded extensively with Red Nichols, Benny Goodman, Fats Waller, Louis Armstrong, Wingy Mannone, and Eddie Condon. He had his own band in the 1940s, but joined Louis Armstrong's All-Stars in July 1947. Teagarden formed his own All-Stars, playing Europe in the 1950s, and co-led a touring sextet with Earl Hines. Teagarden was also much in demand as a vocalist.

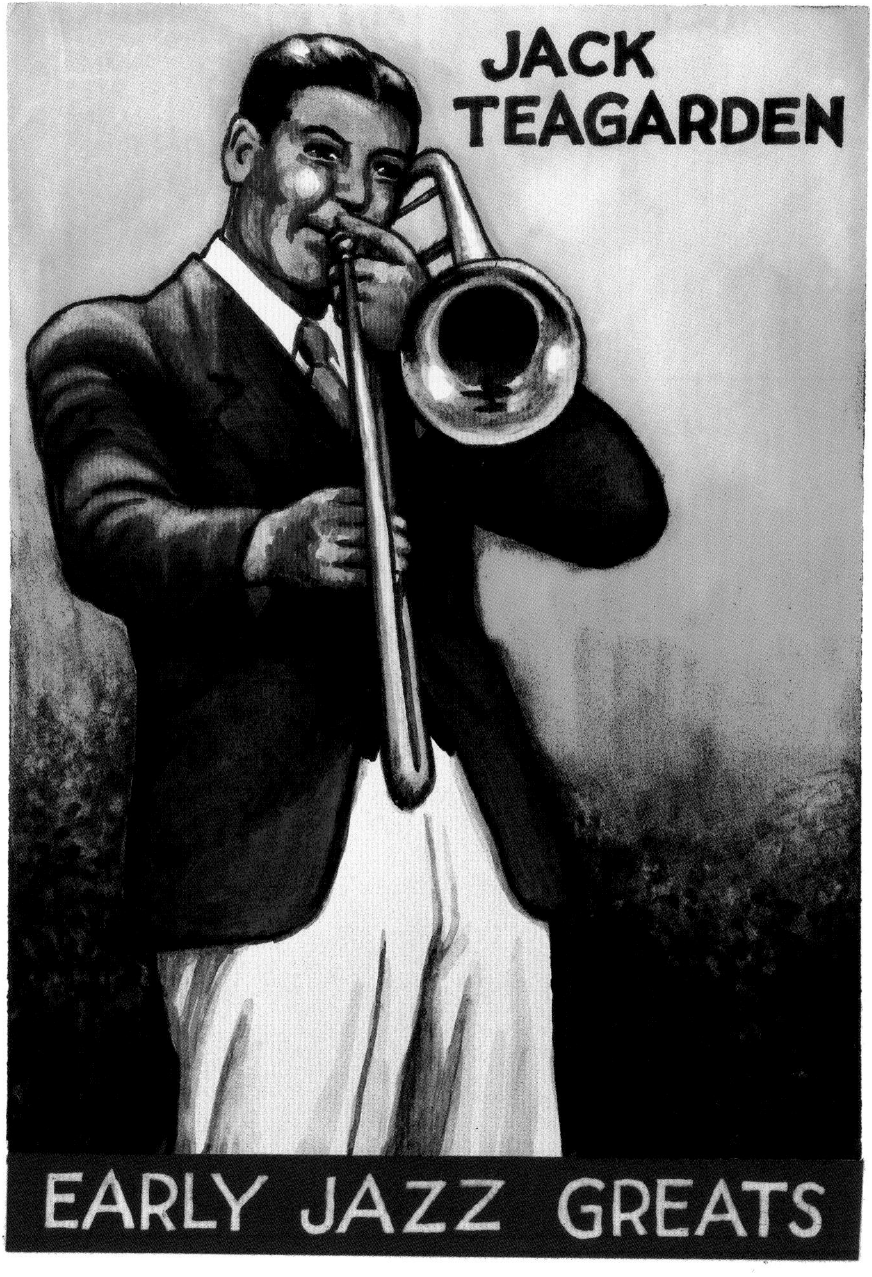
JACK
TEAGARDEN
EARLY JAZZ GREATS

# JABBO SMITH

**TRUMPET**

*B: Pembroke, Georgia, December 24, 1908*
*D: New York, New York, January 16, 1991*

Jabbo Smith was a fine trumpeter whose ability to
imitate Louis Armstrong won him a recording contract
with Brunswick Records. The 1929 recordings of his
Rhythm Aces constituted a high spot in his already
distinguished career. He played with Gus Aiken,
Charlie Johnson, Duke Ellington, James P. Johnson,
Earl "Fatha" Hines, Charlie Elgar, Erskine Tate, Fess
Williams, Tiny Parham, and Claude Hopkins.

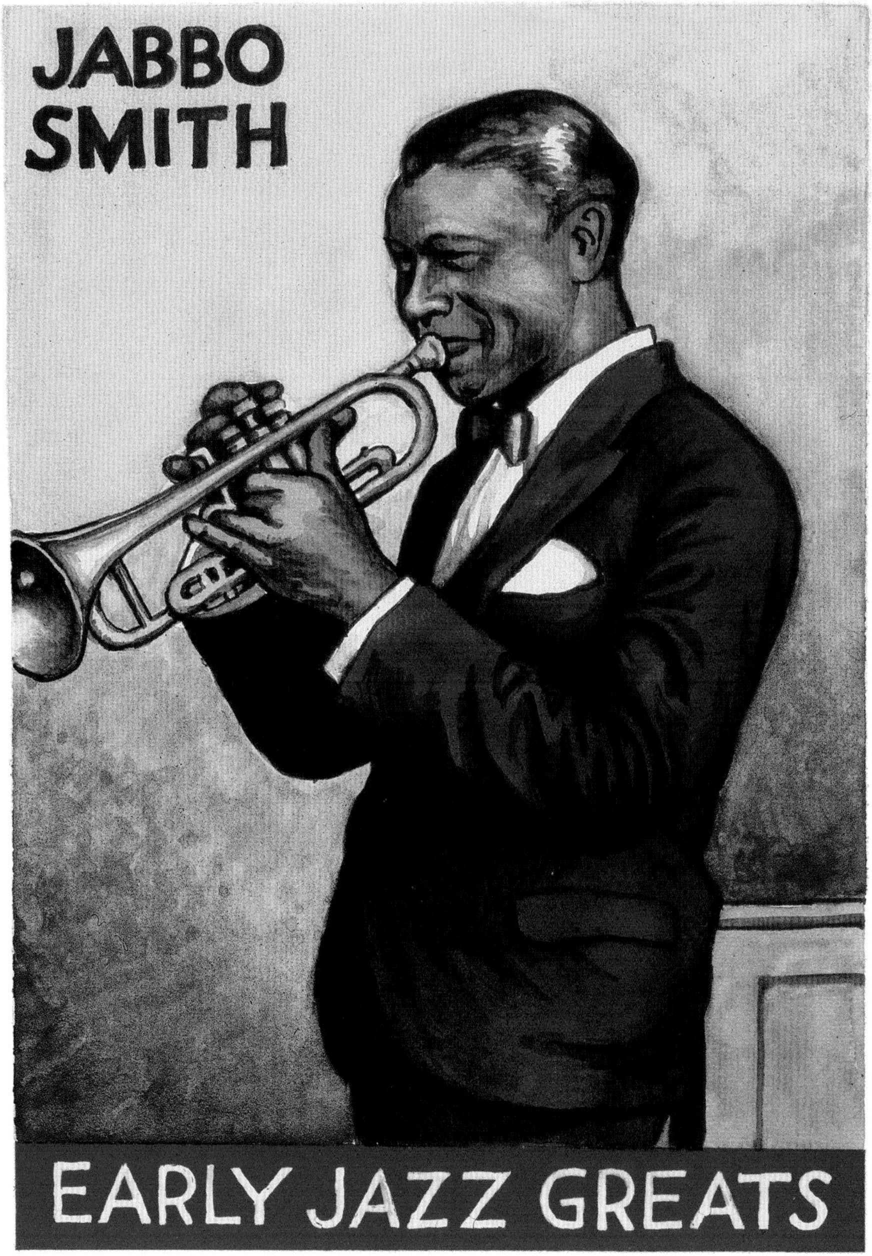
JABBO
SMITH
EARLY JAZZ GREATS

# JOE "WINGY" MANNONE

**TRUMPET**

*B: New Orleans, Louisiana, February 13, 1904*
*D: Las Vegas, Nevada, July 9, 1982*

Joe Mannone lost his right arm when he was eight, and was thereafter known as Wingy. By the age of seventeen he was performing in jazz bands. His first notable band was the Crescent City Jazzers, which became the Arcadian Serenaders when the band made its first recordings in St. Louis in 1924. A disciple of "Bix" Beiderbecke, Mannone played in many bands through-out the far West and South. Following a stint with the dance bands of Ray Miller and Charley Straight in Chicago, Mannone led his own band in New York from 1934. Always on the go, he played major cities until he moved to Hollywood in 1940, where he regularly appeared in films and radio, especially with Bing Crosby. Starting in 1954, he lived and played in Las Vegas. His appearances in the 1960s and '70s were mostly limited to jazz festivals. His autobiography, *Trumpet on the Wing*, was published in 1948.

JOE "WINGY" MANNONE

EARLY JAZZ GREATS

# "POPS" FOSTER

**DOUBLE BASS**
*B: McCall, Louisiana, May 18, 1892*
*D: San Francisco, California, October 30, 1969*

"Pops" Foster began his career on double bass at age
fourteen in New Orleans honky-tonks with the legendary
Jack Carey, Kid Ory, Armand Piron, and Joe "King"
Oliver, and played regularly on the riverboats with Fate
Marable. In St. Louis between 1921 and 1923, Foster
found steady work with Charlie Creath and Dewey
Jackson. Moving to Los Angeles, Foster played with Kid
Ory again and with Mutt Carey. In 1929, he joined Luis
Russell's Orchestra, where he stayed until 1940. He
appeared with Art Hodes and Sidney Bechet in New
York during the mid-1940s, and was a regular on Rudi
Blesh's radio show *This Is Jazz*. Beginning in the early
1960s he toured the country with various groups.

"POPS"
FOSTER

EARLY JAZZ GREATS

# STEVE BROWN

**DOUBLE BASS**
*B: New Orleans, Louisiana, 1890*
*D: Detroit, Michigan, September 15, 1965*

Steve Brown originally played tuba in his brother
Tom's band. He switched to double bass and moved to
Chicago with Tom's band in 1915. In Chicago, Brown
joined the New Orleans Rhythm Kings, and in 1924
teamed with Jean Goldkette until 1927 when he became
part of Paul Whiteman's Orchestra. Brown is best
known for his recordings with "Bix" Beiderbecke in
Goldkette's band and Whiteman's Orchestra.

STEVE
BROWN

EARLY JAZZ GREATS

# EARL HINES

**PIANO**

*B: Pittsburgh, Pennsylvania, December 28, 1903*
*D: Oakland, California, April 22, 1983*

A recording artist who started out in 1923, Earl "Fatha" Hines made his first piano solos in December 1928. Gaining national recognition through his recordings with Louis Armstrong's Hot Five, Hines continued with Jimmy Noone and throughout the 1930s recorded with his own Grand Terrace Orchestra. Hines rejoined Armstrong at the beginning of 1948 and stayed with the All-Stars until late 1951. Throughout the 1950s and 1960s, Hines toured Europe with various all-star groups. After the 1970s he played clubs and festivals either as a soloist or with his quartet. His influence was felt in the big-band era as pianists modified his style to suit the requirements of the swing age.

EARL
HINES

EARLY JAZZ GREATS

# JIMMY BLYTHE

**PIANO**

*B: Lexington, Kentucky, c. 1901*
*D: Chicago, Illinois, June 14, 1931*

James "Jimmy" Blythe moved to Chicago in 1915, where
he was given piano lessons by Clarence Jones. Blythe
had an extremely active recording career from his debut
for Paramount Records in 1924 until his untimely death
from meningitis in 1931. He led six groups, played piano
with eleven others, and accompanied a dozen blues
singers. For his own groups he used such outstanding
jazzmen as Freddie Keppard, Louis Armstrong, Johnny
Dodds, and Natty Dominique. His nine piano solos and
four duets can't compare in numbers with the more
than two hundred piano rolls he made for the Capitol
Roll Company, many of which were pop tunes, a genre
missing from his recorded output.

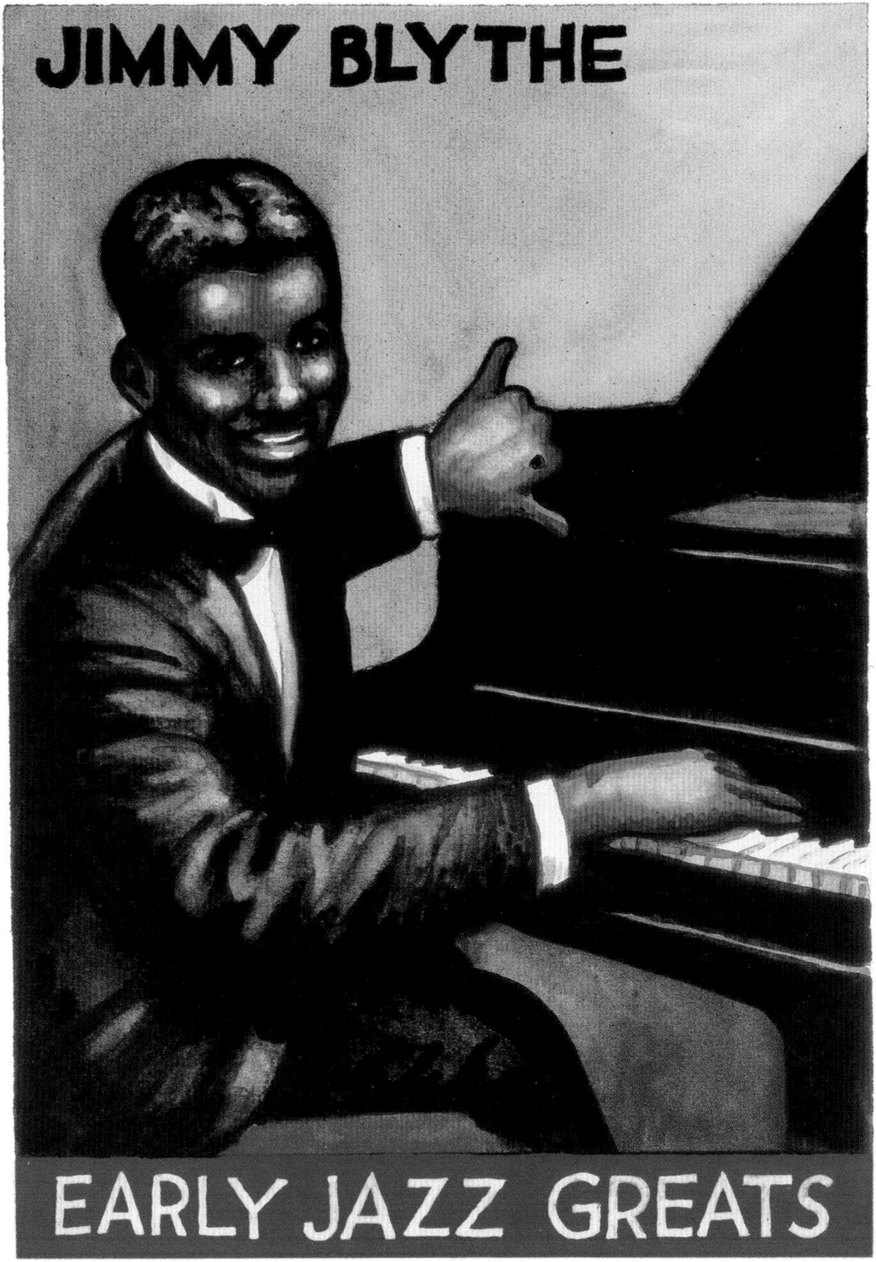
JIMMY BLYTHE
EARLY JAZZ GREATS

# JAMES P. JOHNSON

**PIANO**

*B: New Brunswick, New Jersey, February 1, 1891*
*D: Jamaica, New York, November 17, 1955*

Known as the Father of the Stride Piano, Jimmy
Johnson established himself as the premier rent-party
pianist. With such original rags as "Carolina Shout,"
"Daintiness Rag," "Caprice Rag," and "Harlem Strut,"
Johnson became the first famous black piano roll
arranger and performer. While he played the most
respected clubs in Harlem — Barron Wilkin's, Leroy's,
the Clef Club — Johnson also toured the Midwest. He
composed scores for Broadway shows, including such
songs as "If I Could Be With You," "Old Fashioned
Love," and the archetypal song and dance of the Roaring
Twenties, "The Charleston." His most famous recording was his own composition "Snowy Morning Blues,"
recorded for Columbia Records in 1927.

JAMES P. JOHNSON

EARLY JAZZ GREATS

# "TINY" PARHAM

**PIANO, ARRANGER**
*B: Winnipeg, Canada, February 25, 1900*
*D: Milwaukee, Wisconsin, April 4, 1943*

Hartzell "Tiny" Parham grew up in Kansas City and
got his first job at the Eblon Theater under the direction
of ragtime composer James Scott. In 1926 Parham
moved to Chicago, where he formed his own band and
recorded extensively for Victor Records, whose good
fidelity sound allowed his fine jazz piano to be heard.
At times, bluesman Papa Charlie Jackson would play
banjo in Parham's band. From the mid-1930s Parham
performed on the organ at theaters, movie houses, and
skating rinks.

"TINY" PARHAM

EARLY JAZZ GREATS

# "DUKE" ELLINGTON

**PIANO, ARRANGER**
*B: Washington, D.C., April 28, 1899*
*D: New York, New York, May 24, 1974*

An outstanding triple-threat jazzman equally at home
as composer, bandleader, and arranger, Edward
Kennedy "Duke" Ellington learned piano from James
P. Johnson's piano roll of "Carolina Shout." His first
band, the Washingtonians (organized in 1923) included
Bubber Miley, Charlie Irvis, Otto Hardwick, Fred Guy,
and Sonny Greer. They were to remain with him for life.
His recording debut for Blu-Disc in 1924 began an
incredibly prolific recording career that was to last until
his death. His compositions, including "Mood Indigo,"
"Solitude," "Sophisticated Lady," "I Got It Bad," and
"It Don't Mean a Thing," remain pop and jazz standards.
His band's theme song, "Take the A Train" (composed
in 1941 by his collaborator Billy Strayhorn), was his first
record to sell a million copies.

"DUKE" ELLINGTON

EARLY JAZZ GREATS

# SIDNEY BECHET

**CLARINET, SOPRANO SAXOPHONE**
*B: New Orleans, Louisiana, May 14, 1897*
*D: Paris, France, May 14, 1959*

As a child, Sidney Bechet taught himself the clarinet, sat in with Freddie Keppard, and marched with Manuel Perez. Later Bechet took lessons from the clarinet giants of New Orleans: Lorenzo Tio, Jr., Louis Nelson, and George Baquet. In 1917 Bechet moved to Chicago, where he played with Keppard, Joe "King" Oliver, and Tony Jackson. In 1919, Bechet bought a soprano saxophone and became its premier practitioner in jazz. His presence on recordings is easily confirmed by his wide-vibrato sound. From 1932 to 1941 his seven-piece group, the New Orleans Feetwarmers, recorded extensively for Victor Records. In 1940, he made eight sides with Muggsy Spanier.

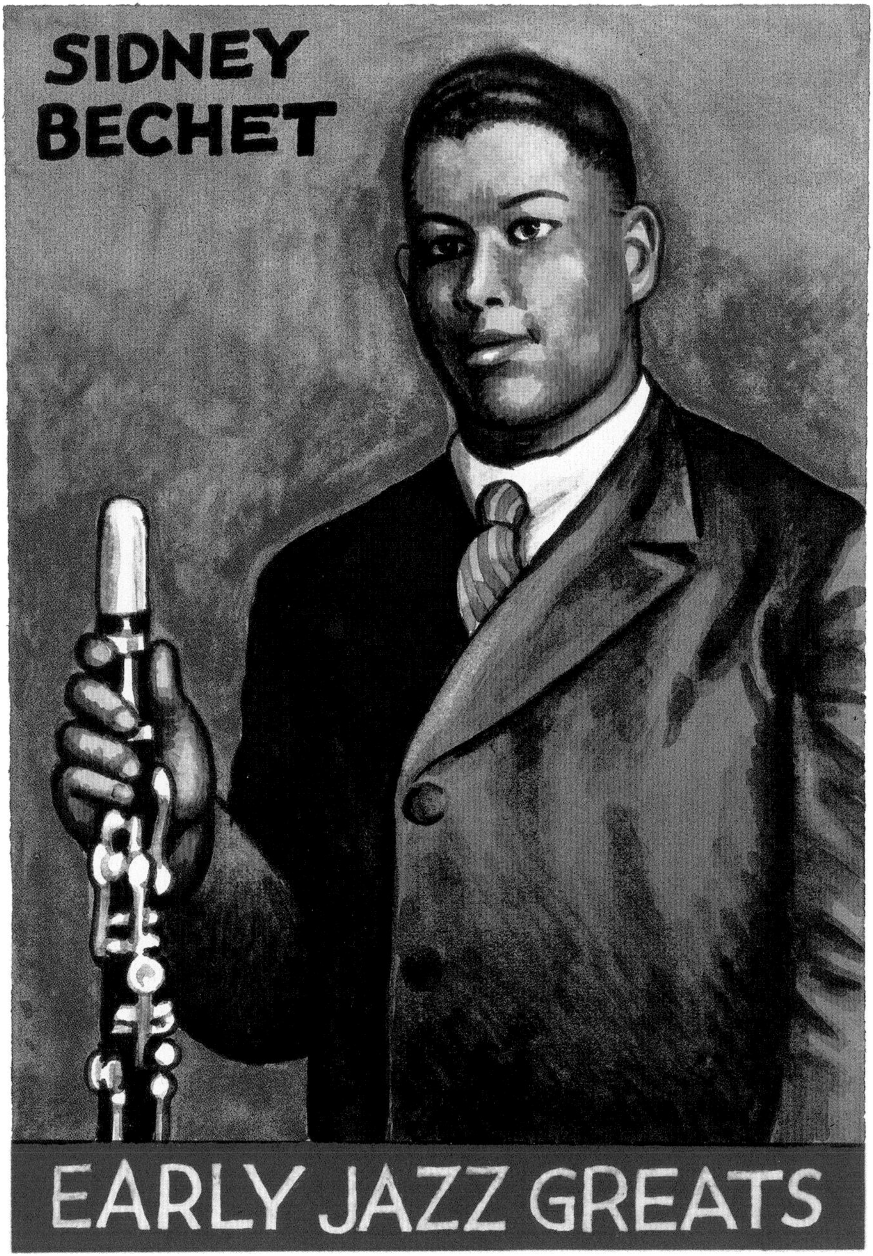
SIDNEY
BECHET
EARLY JAZZ GREATS

# FREDDIE KEPPARD

**CORNET**

*B: New Orleans, Louisiana, February 15, 1889*
*D: Chicago, Illinois, July 15, 1933*

A pioneer jazz cornetist who organized the Olympia
Orchestra around 1906, Freddie Keppard also worked
in Frankie Dusen's Eagle Band. At the request of bassist
Bill Johnson, Keppard became co-leader of the Original
Creole Orchestra, which toured the Orpheum Circuit
in vaudeville, until 1918, when he settled in Chicago.
He worked with Doc Cooke, Erskine Tate, Jimmy Noone,
Ollie Powers, and Charlie Elgar. Keppard's sweet yet
sure tones were faithfully captured on his Okeh,
Columbia, and Gennett Records, sessions with Doc
Cooke's Gingersnaps (1926) and with the Dreamland
Orchestra (1924–27).

FREDDIE KEPPARD

EARLY JAZZ GREATS

# THOMAS "FATS" WALLER

**PIANO**

B: *New York, New York, May 21, 1904*
D: *Kansas City, Kansas, December 15, 1943*

A protégé of stride pianist James P. Johnson, Thomas "Fats" Waller became the most famous jazz pianist of his time through more than one thousand recordings, a weekly network radio program, film appearances, worldwide concertizing, and nightclub performances in the United States. He composed more than three thousand songs — several becoming standards — including "Ain't Misbehavin'," "Honeysuckle Rose," "I've Got a Feeling I'm Fallin'," and "Blue Turning Grey Over You."

# THOMAS "FATS" WALLER

## EARLY JAZZ GREATS

# "MUGGSY" SPANIER

**CORNET**

*B: Chicago, Illinois, November 9, 1906*
*D: Sausalito, California, February 12, 1967*

Francis Julian "Muggsy" Spanier began playing the
cornet at age thirteen and had his first professional
engagement with Sig Meyers's Band in 1923. Early in
the next year, Spanier made his recording debut with
his own group, the Bucktown Five. Influenced by both
"Bix" Beiderbecke and Louis Armstrong, Spanier
developed a distinctive, driving style that enhanced the
bands of Ray Miller, Ted Lewis, Ben Pollack, and Bob
Crosby. With his own Ragtimers, Spanier made a series
of classic recordings in 1939. He led his own bands
and guest-starred in others, appearing at jazz festivals
throughout the world.

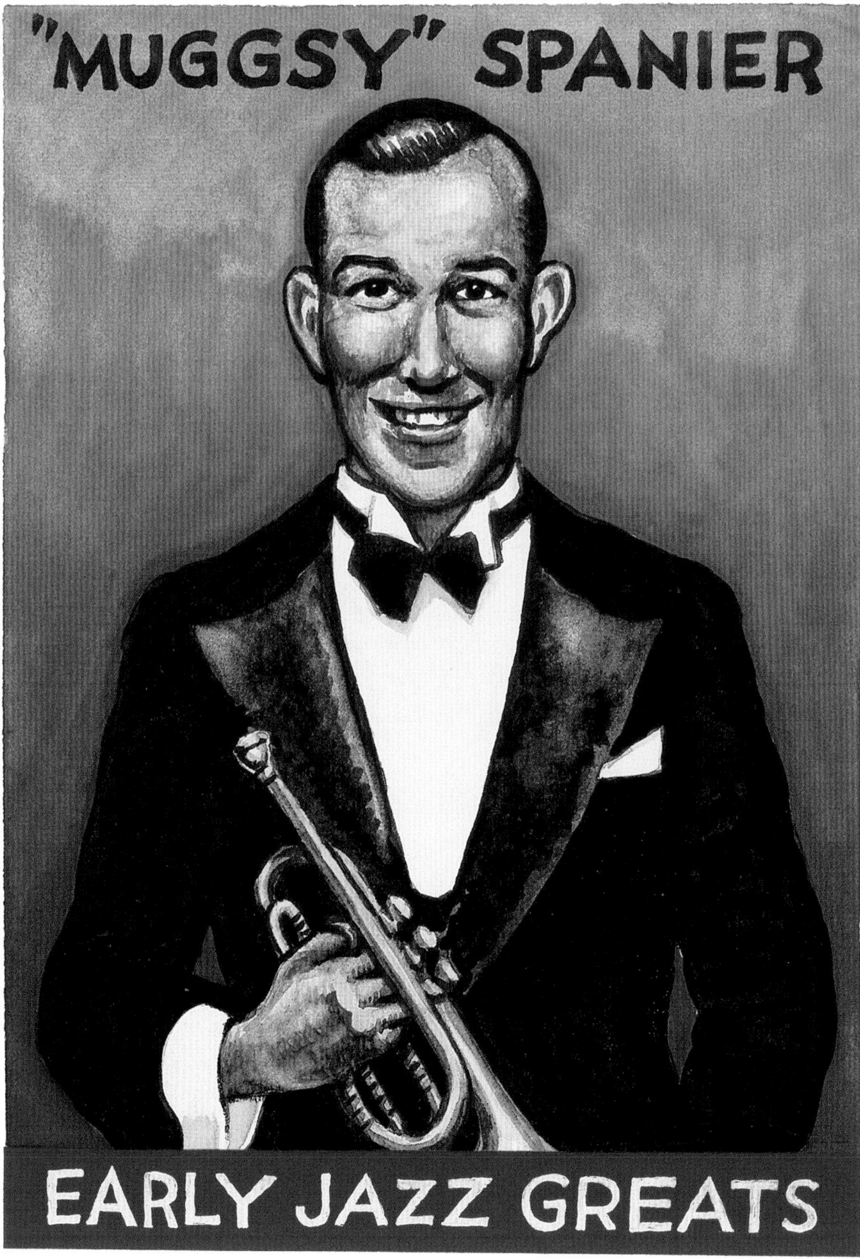
"MUGGSY" SPANIER
EARLY JAZZ GREATS

# LAMMAR WRIGHT

**CORNET**
*B: Texarkana, Texas, June 20, 1907*
*D: New York, New York, April 13, 1973*

Lammar Wright gained initial fame as the trumpeter
with the Bennie Moten Orchestra in 1923, and his
bandmates included the Missourians (whom he joined
in 1927), Cab Calloway, Don Redman, Claude Hopkins,
Cootie Williams, Lucky Millinder, Sy Oliver, and George
Shearing. Starting in the late 1940s with the formation
of his own studio, Wright became one of New York's
great trumpet teachers. He made countless recordings
in big bands and as a studio musician.

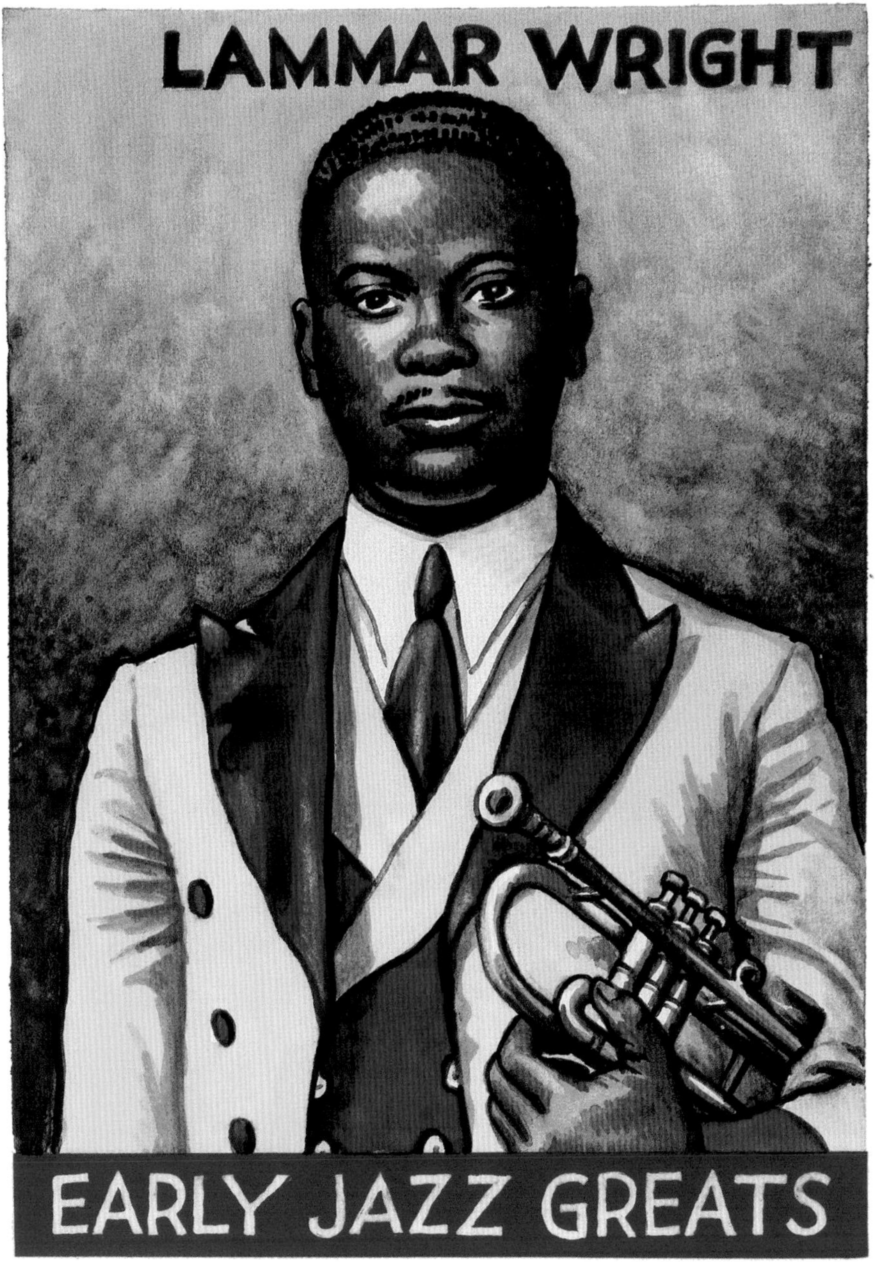
LAMMAR WRIGHT
EARLY JAZZ GREATS

# BENNIE MOTEN

**PIANO, ARRANGER**
*B: Kansas City, Missouri, November 13, 1894*
*D: Kansas City, Missouri, April 2, 1935*

This multi-talented jazzman organized his own
Dixieland band at the start of the Roaring Twenties.
In 1923 Moten began making a series of recordings
destined to spread his fame as a pianist-composer-
arranger. By 1927 his ensemble had grown to a big
band, and his Victor recordings catapulted him to
national fame. "South," his most famous recording,
sold millions. His unusual arrangements and highly
talented band members (including Lammar Wright,
Woody Walder, Harlan Leonard, Eddie Durham,
and Count Basie) made his an outstanding band.

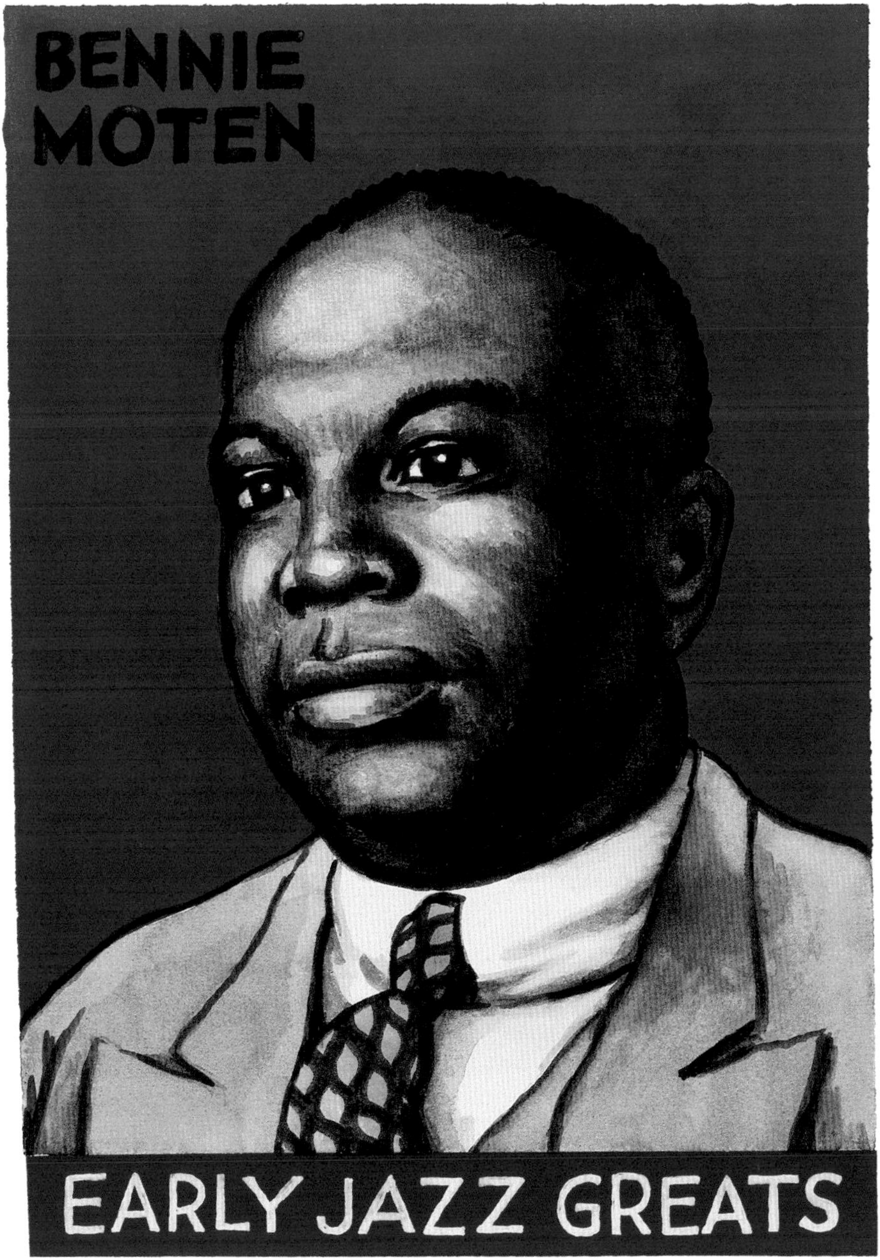
BENNIE
MOTEN
EARLY JAZZ GREATS

# FRANK TRUMBAUER

**C–MELODY SAXOPHONE**
*B: Carbondale, Illinois, May 30, 1901*
*D: Kansas City, Missouri, June 11, 1956*

Frank Trumbauer grew up in St. Louis, where he studied the piano, trombone, violin, and flute. He played with various local bands until he joined the famous Gene Rodemich Orchestra, with whom he made his recording debut in 1922 on the ubiquitous C–melody saxophone. He then joined Ray Miller's Orchestra in Chicago before moving to Jean Goldkette's organization as music director of the band, which included "Bix" Beiderbecke. Beiderbecke was a close associate, and both joined Paul Whiteman's Orchestra at the end of 1927, making many recordings together.

FRANK TRUMBAUER

EARLY JAZZ GREATS

# MARY LOU WILLIAMS

**PIANO, ARRANGER**
*B: Atlanta, Georgia, May 8, 1910*
*D: Durham, North Carolina, May 28, 1981*

Like Earl "Fatha" Hines, Mary Lou Williams was a
remarkable jazz pianist who was able to develop
pianistically and change styles every decade. She married
saxophonist John Williams in 1928 and played in his
band. Both joined Terrence Holder's Band, which
became Andy Kirk's Twelve Clouds of Joy. Williams
became the band's arranger as well as pianist. She also
arranged for Benny Goodman, Duke Ellington, Tommy
Dorsey, Louis Armstrong, and Glen Gray. Williams
toured Europe extensively and had many long engage-
ments in New York. Her recording debut for Paramount
Records in 1927 began a studio career that lasted
until her death.

# MARY LOU WILLIAMS

## EARLY JAZZ GREATS

# ERNEST "PUNCH" MILLER

**CORNET**

*B: Raceland, Louisiana, June 14, 1894*
*D: New Orleans, Louisiana, December 2, 1971*

Ernest "Punch" Miller played bass drums, baritone horn, and trombone before deciding on cornet, which he played with Kid Ory and Jack Carey in New Orleans in the 1910s. Moving to Chicago in the mid-1920s, he toured with "Jelly Roll" Morton, Albert Wynn, "Tiny" Parham, and Erskine Tate. He played in New Orleans from 1965 until his death.

ERNEST "PUNCH" MILLER

EARLY JAZZ GREATS

# EDDIE SOUTH

**VIOLIN**

*B: Louisiana, Missouri, November 27, 1904*
*D: Chicago, Illinois, April 25, 1962*

Eddie South grew up in Chicago, where he studied
with Charlie Elgar and Darnell Howard. Working with
Elgar and Erskine Tate, South led Jimmy Wade's
Syncopators at the Moulin Rouge Café from 1924 to
1927. South toured Europe with his own group, the
Alabamians, throughout the 1930s. His recording
debut for Paramount Records in 1923 was with Wade's
band. South continued recording for various companies until 1958. He returned to Chicago in the 1950s,
appearing on his own television shows where he was
billed as the Dark Angel of the Violin.

EDDIE
SOUTH

EARLY JAZZ GREATS

# ALEX HILL

**PIANO, ARRANGER**
*B: Little Rock, Arkansas, April 19, 1906*
*D: Little Rock, Arkansas, February 1937*

Alex Hill first became known to Chicago jazz circles when he was about twenty-one. He played and arranged for such diverse artists as Jimmy Wade, Carroll Dickerson, Ernest "Punch" Miller, Albert Wynn, and Jimmy Noone. Hill made only a few recordings under his own name in late 1929 and early 1930. Upon moving to the San Francisco Bay Area, he arranged for the highly respected Paul Howard's Quality Serenaders. Hill spent most of his remaining life struggling with alcoholism in New York; composing pop tunes for Mills Music, Inc.; and arranging for such outstanding bands led by Paul Whiteman, Claude Hopkins, and Duke Ellington. Tuberculosis forced Hill to retire to his brother's home in Little Rock, where he died.

ALEX
HILL

EARLY JAZZ GREATS

# JOE VENUTI

**VIOLIN**

*B: Aboard ship from Italy to the United States, 1903*
*D: Seattle, Washington, August 14, 1976*

Joe Venuti was raised in Philadelphia to become a
professional violinist. His classical training led to his
superb technique and flawless intonation. Venuti
and guitarist Eddie Lang met as schoolmates in 1915
and started playing professionally together in 1918, an
association that lasted until Lang's death in 1933. Venuti
started out by infusing ethnic polkas and mazurkas with
a jazz orientation, and as he expanded more fully into
jazz melodies, his great instrumental fluency permitted
him to improvise extensively. Venuti recorded with some
of the big names in jazz, notably "Bix" Beiderbecke,
and surrounded himself in his own groups with such
talented instrumentalists as Frank Signorelli, Adrian
Rollini, Benny Goodman, and Tommy and Jimmy
Dorsey. Venuti's technical acuity and musical inven-
tiveness continued even into his last years.

JOE
VENUTI

EARLY JAZZ GREATS

# FLETCHER HENDERSON

**PIANO, ARRANGER**
*B: Cuthbert, Georgia, December 18, 1897*
*D: New York, New York, December 28, 1952*

Fletcher Henderson went to New York in 1920, where
he became a song plugger for the Pace & Handy Music
Co. When Harry Pace left to become the first black
entrepreneur to form a recording company, Black Swan
Records, Henderson became its recording director and
house orchestra leader. From 1924 to 1934 his band
played at Roseland Ballroom, New York's number–one
dance hall. Recording regularly from 1921, he was a
pioneer in that he was the first leader–arranger to break
up his orchestra into sections, playing one against
another for tonal contrast. His greatest achievement
was in creating the swing era sound of Benny
Goodman's Orchestra.

FLETCHER
HENDERSON

EARLY JAZZ GREATS

# JIMMY NOONE

**CLARINET, ALTO SAXOPHONE**
B: *Cut-Off, Louisiana, April 23, 1895*
D: *Los Angeles, California, April 19, 1944*

One of the all-time great clarinetists and alto
saxophonists, Jimmy Noone studied under Sidney
Bechet, whom he replaced in Freddie Keppard's band
in 1913 for his first professional appearance. Noone
played with Kid Ory, King Oliver, and Doc Cooke's
Dreamland Orchestra, making a series of recordings
with Earl "Fatha" Hines in 1928. Noone continued to
record with his own orchestra throughout the 1930s.
He appeared on radio and with the Bowery Boys in the
Monogram Pictures film *Block Busters* (1944) just
before he died.

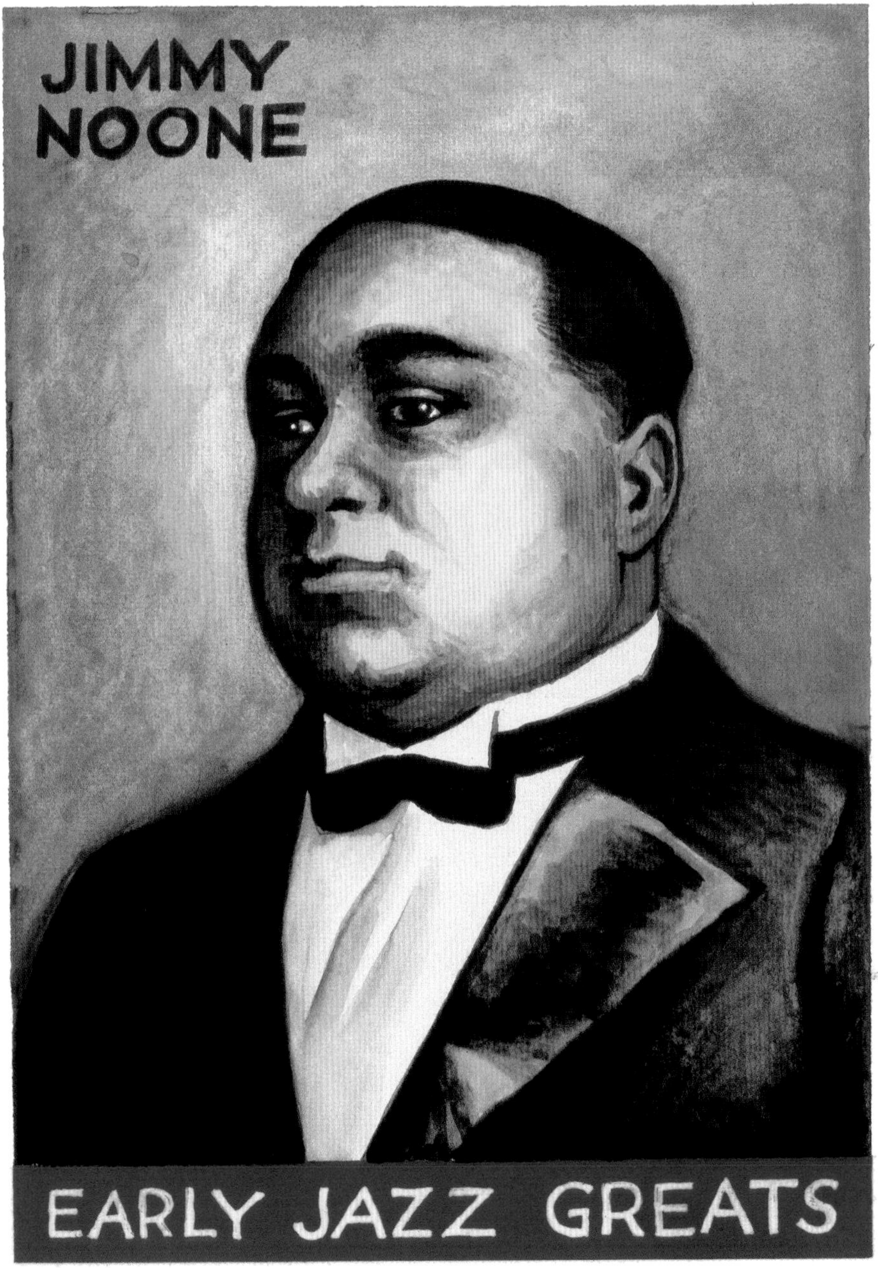
JIMMY
NOONE
EARLY JAZZ GREATS

# BENNY GOODMAN

**CLARINET**
*B: Chicago, Illinois, May 30, 1909*
*D: New York, New York, June 13, 1986*

Benny Goodman studied clarinet at age twelve, and began his professional career one year later. Playing at Guyon's Paradise and Midway Gardens, he then signed with Ben Pollack in 1925 where (with interruptions) Goodman remained until 1929 when he became a freelancer in New York. There he performed on radio, in Broadway pit bands, and on recordings. His first band was created in 1934 and was heard on the network radio show *Let's Dance*, where he was billed as the King of Swing. His phenomenal initial success was due to Fletcher Henderson's arrangements. Goodman's first big record hit was Henderson's arrangement of "Jelly Roll" Morton's "King Porter Stomp" in 1935.

BENNY GOODMAN

EARLY JAZZ GREATS

# ANDY PALMER OF JIMMIE JOHNSON'S STRING BAND

**FIDDLE**

*B: c. 1881*

*D: c. 1929*

Andy Palmer of Anderson County, Kentucky, ranks as the perfect prototype of an old-time traditional fiddler. His eminently exciting dynamics defined by brilliantly controlled crescendos of volume and a brisk, articulate attack set Palmer in a class by himself. Add his uncanny, innate sense of syncopation and Palmer becomes a premier dance fiddler. It's difficult to sit still when listening to Palmer's masterful work on his only recorded selections — eight sides for the Champion Records label published in 1932 with Jimmie Johnson's String Band. These 78s are among the rarest of all early country recordings. There is only one surviving copy of each of his three records, one of which sold a mere 99 copies. His fourth record has never been found. Born about 1881, Palmer worked as a brakeman for the L & N Railroad, as well as being a professional musician during his forty-eight-year lifetime. Although relatively unknown until recently, he is now recognized as a giant figure in early American music.

**ANDY PALMER of JIMMIE JOHNSON'S STRING BAND**

# ECK ROBERTSON AND FAMILY

| **Eck Robertson** | **Dueron Robertson** | **Nettie Robertson** | **Daphne Robertson** |
|---|---|---|---|
| FIDDLE | BANJO | GUITAR | TENOR GUITAR |
| B: *Delaney, Arkansas, November 20, 1887* | B: *Unknown* | B: *Unknown* | B: *Unknown* |
| D: *Borger, Texas, February 15, 1975* | D: *Unknown* | D: *Unknown* | D: *Unknown* |

Considered by many to be the finest fiddler of the whole era of early recorded country music, Alexander Campbell "Eck" Robertson was born in 1887 in Delaney, Arkansas. His family moved to Amarillo, Texas, when he was three years old, and he spent the rest of his life there. The fiddling tradition was especially rich in Texas; the standard of playing being perhaps the highest in the United States. From this rich setting, Robertson learned all the diverse styles of early American fiddle music and, incredibly, became master of them all. His first record, "Sally Gooden," made in 1922, was a landmark as it was the first commercial recording of traditional American music. More than eighty-five years later it still inspires awe for its seemingly impossible technique

and brilliant array of variations. It is also the best representation of the oldest style of American fiddling extant: an archaic cross-tuned, open-string A tuning (E–A–E–A) in which constant drones are used and in which it is possible to play the melody in two separate octaves. Robertson was equally adept at playing very syncopated dance tunes, ragtime pieces, long bow, melodically intricate contest numbers, smooth uptown waltzes, blues tunes, and even backup fiddling. The only other figure who could claim such total command of the whole spectrum of American fiddle music was Ed Haley of Kentucky, an artist of the same giant stature as Robertson himself. Robertson recorded fourteen selections for Victor, many of which featured backup by his wife and children.

ECK ROBERTSON
AND FAMILY

# DA COSTA WOLTZ'S SOUTHERN BROADCASTERS

### Da Costa Woltz
LEAD BANJO
B: *Surry County,*
*North Carolina*
D: *Unknown*

### Frank Jenkins
BANJO
B: *Surry County,*
*North Carolina, 1888*
D: *Unknown*

### Ben Jarrell
FIDDLE, VOCALS
B: *Surry County,*
*North Carolina, 1880*
D: *Unknown*

### Price Goodson
HARMONICA,
UKULELE, VOCALS
B: *c. 1915*
D: *Unknown*

The totally distinct sound of Da Costa Woltz's Southern Broadcasters was the product of their unusual instrumental interplay of fiddle and two banjos. The lead banjo, played by Da Costa Woltz in open tuning, had a highly developed melody line, and used a two-finger, thumb-lead style similar to that of Marion Underwood of Kentucky. The second banjo, played in standard tuning by Frank Jenkins, had a more sophisticated style that used chording and three-finger picking. Both these virtuoso musicians had complete command of their playing, and their brilliant ensemble sound was at the heart of the band's music. The complete melody line was provided by Ben Jarrell on fiddle and vocals. Jarrell was a powerful fiddler who played in a syncopated style that featured a constantly rolling bow that rhythmically accentuated each note. A perfect complement to the double banjos, his driving fiddling and singing were both in a very high register. These three Surry County, North Carolina, natives formed the nucleus of the band. For three of the band's eighteen selections (recorded at one session in 1927 for Gennett), it was accompanied by Price Goodson, a twelve-year-old who played harmonica and ukulele, and sang. Also recorded during this session were individual band members' specialties, such as Jenkins's banjo solo of "Home Sweet Home" and Woltz's masterful "John Brown's Dream," the finest clawhammer banjo effort of the period. Jenkins was also a gifted fiddler. His "Sunny Home in Dixie," recorded in 1929, provides a showcase for his smooth, gutsy, legato playing and his broad, deep tone. Although called the Broadcasters, the band never appeared on radio, and stayed together only a short time.

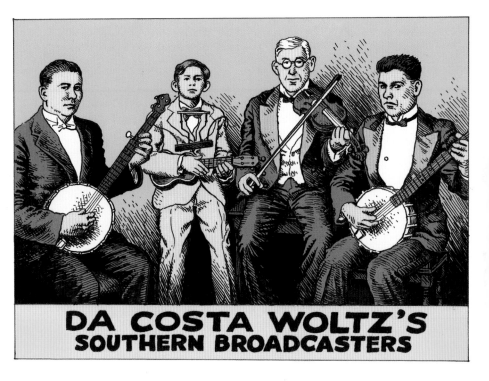

# DA COSTA WOLTZ'S
## SOUTHERN BROADCASTERS

# GID TANNER AND HIS SKILLET LICKERS

| James Gideon (Gid) Tanner | George Riley Puckett | Clayton McMichen | Lowe Stokes | Fate Norris |
|---|---|---|---|---|
| FIDDLE | GUITAR, VOCALS | FIDDLE | FIDDLE | BANJO |
| B: *Thomas Bridge, Georgia, June 6, 1885* | B: *Alpharetta, Georgia, May 7, 1894* | B: *Allatoona, Georgia, January 26, 1900* | B: *Unknown* | B: *Unknown* |
| D: *Dacula, Georgia, May 13, 1960* | D: *Georgia, July 14, 1946* | D: *Battlesboro, Kentucky, January 4, 1970* | D: *Unknown* | D: *Unknown* |

The most famous fiddle band of the 1920s was the Skillet Lickers of northern Georgia. The lineup for the 1920s Columbia Records sides comprising most of the group's work was Lowe Stokes, Clayton McMichen, Bert Layne, and James Gideon (Gid) Tanner on fiddles, George Riley Puckett on guitar and vocals, and Fate Norris on banjo. Fiddling for the 1930s Bluebird Records sessions was done by Gid Tanner and his son, Gordon. Stokes's clean, articulate phrasing and exquisite tone (the product of his long, smooth bowing) made him one of the finest recorded fiddlers. Together with the proficient McMichen, their unison and harmony fiddling was the heart of the Skillet Lickers' music. One of the most popular vocalists of the period, Puckett played backup guitar in a very influential bass note run style. Barely passable as a musician, Tanner, the organizer of the band, provided comic relief. The group was prolific, recording more than a hundred sides for Columbia and Bluebird. The band's best efforts feature superb, hard-driving twin and triple fiddling, both polished for its smooth, mellow tone and exciting in its pure traditional power.

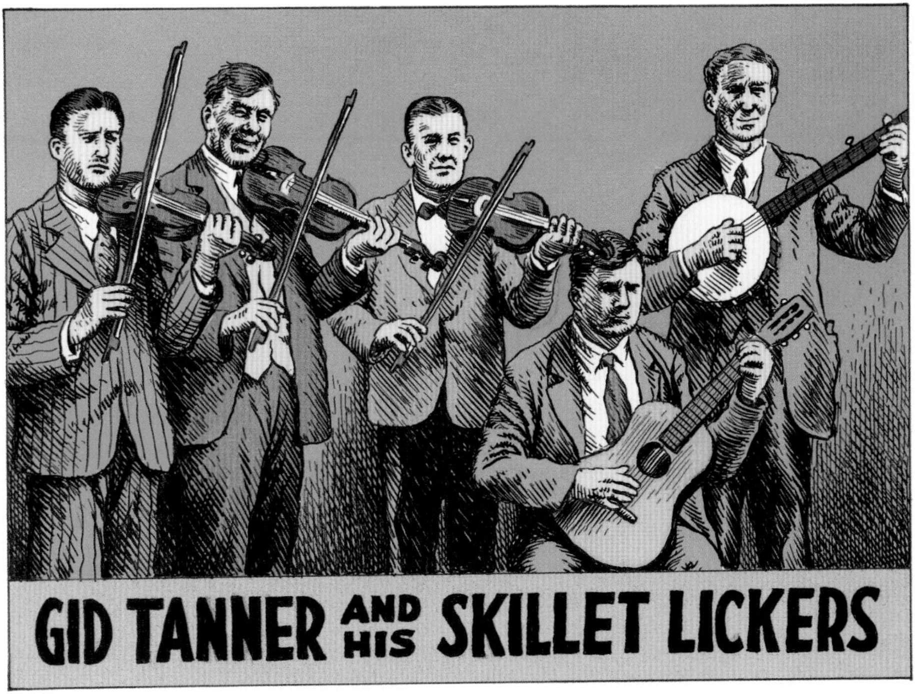
GID TANNER AND HIS SKILLET LICKERS

# FIDDLIN' JOHN CARSON
# & HIS VIRGINIA REELERS

**Fiddlin' John Carson**
FIDDLE
B: *Blue Ridge, Fannin County, Georgia, March 23, 1868*
D: *December 11, 1949*

**T. M. Brewer**
FIDDLE
B: *Unknown*
D: *Unknown*

**Rosa Lee**
GUITAR
B: *Unknown*
D: *Unknown*

Fiddlin' John Carson was one of the foremost pioneers in the early commercial recording of country music. His 1922 recording of "Little Old Log Cabin in the Lane" was the first real country music record. Almost single-handedly it convinced record companies that this music could be sold profitably to a purely rural audience. This conclusion was the basis of commercial country music. Carson was steeped in both the older styles of fiddling with their specialized open tunings and the larger repertoires that were common to that earlier period. Although somewhat rough in attack, his fiddling was appealing for its syncopation and the resonant tone that was frequently augmented by the drone strings of his open tunings. Carson had some of the finest versions of tunes and his performances abounded with novel twists and turns of rhythm and phrasing. He was expert in the old traditional style of backing his vocal with his own fiddle. Carson's best recordings were his 1927 selections with the Virginia Reelers, whose other members were Earl Johnson and T. M. Brewer on fiddles (in this illustration T. M. is shown on the right, playing guitar); daughter Rosa Lee ("Moon-shine Kate") and Peanuts Brown on guitars (Rosa, pictured here on the left, is shown playing banjo); and Bill White on banjo. These are among the most exciting and delightful performances of the whole period. There are a few recordings on which Carson seems more than a little soused, and these are, depending on your perspective, either quite funny or quite sad. Carson recorded more than 125 titles, mostly for Okeh Records.

**FIDDLIN' JOHN CARSON & his VIRGINIA REELERS**

# EARL JOHNSON AND HIS DIXIE ENTERTAINERS

### Earl Johnson
**FIDDLE**
B: *Gwinnett County,*
*Georgia, 1886*
D: *Lawrenceville,*
*Georgia, 1965*

### Byrd Moore
**GUITAR**
B: *Unknown*
D: *Unknown*

### Emmett Bankston
**BANJO**
B: *Unknown*
D: *Unknown*

Born in 1886 in Gwinnett County, Georgia, Earl Johnson was easily the wildest fiddler ever to record. Although not a great fiddler or singer, his break-neck speed, exhilarating dynamics, and vocal pyrotechnics charmed his audiences during his fifty-plus years as a professional old-time musician and continue to endear him to each new generation of listeners. Johnson first recorded for Paramount Records with Arthur Tanner's group and also did three records for Victor. His really classic sides were recorded for Okeh Records, both with his own Dixie Entertainers, his Clodhoppers, and John Carson's Virginia Reelers. These titles are outstanding for their two- and three-fiddle arrangements in which Johnson played a high second fiddle. The group was as tight and cohesive as any recorded, due in no small part to the great backup work of Byrd Moore and Red Henderson on guitars and Emmett Bankston on banjo, who contributed immensely to Johnson's success.

EARL JOHNSON AND HIS
DIXIE ENTERTAINERS

# CARTER FAMILY

| Maybelle Addington Carter | A. P. Carter | Sara Dougherty Carter |
|---|---|---|
| **GUITAR** | **ARRANGER, HARMONY** | **VOCALS, GUITAR, AUTOHARP** |
| B: *Nickelsville, Virginia, May 10, 1909* | B: *Maces Spring, Scott County, Virginia, December 15, 1891* | B: *Flatwoods, Virginia, July 21, 1898* |
| D: *October 23, 1978* | D: *November 7, 1960* | D: *January 8, 1979* |

The almost three hundred songs the Carter Family recorded from 1927 to 1941 make up the most formidable body of traditional American balladry, and represent collectively (with the possible exception of Jimmie Rodgers) the most influential performances of the period. Maybelle Addington Carter's distinctive thumb-lead guitar style, esteemed and imitated by count-less country music luminaries for more than seventy-five years, and the Carter Family's vocal stylings greatly contrib-uted to the early development of bluegrass. From Maces Springs, Scott County, in far western Virginia, A. P. Carter was the arranger and sometime harmony singer of the group. Sara Dougherty (A. P.'s wife) was the family's great lead singer and added second guitar and autoharp. The Carter Family's records sold very well, and the group was one of the few early stars on the new country music scene. The first year or two of the Carter Family's recordings (for Victor — they later recorded for ARC Records and Decca) produced some of the finest performances of traditional American song. Sara's then very high-register singing, with its great projection and compellingly plaintive quality, was unrivaled, and Maybelle's brilliant guitar playing perfectly captured all the insistent dynamics of traditional clawhammer banjo styles.

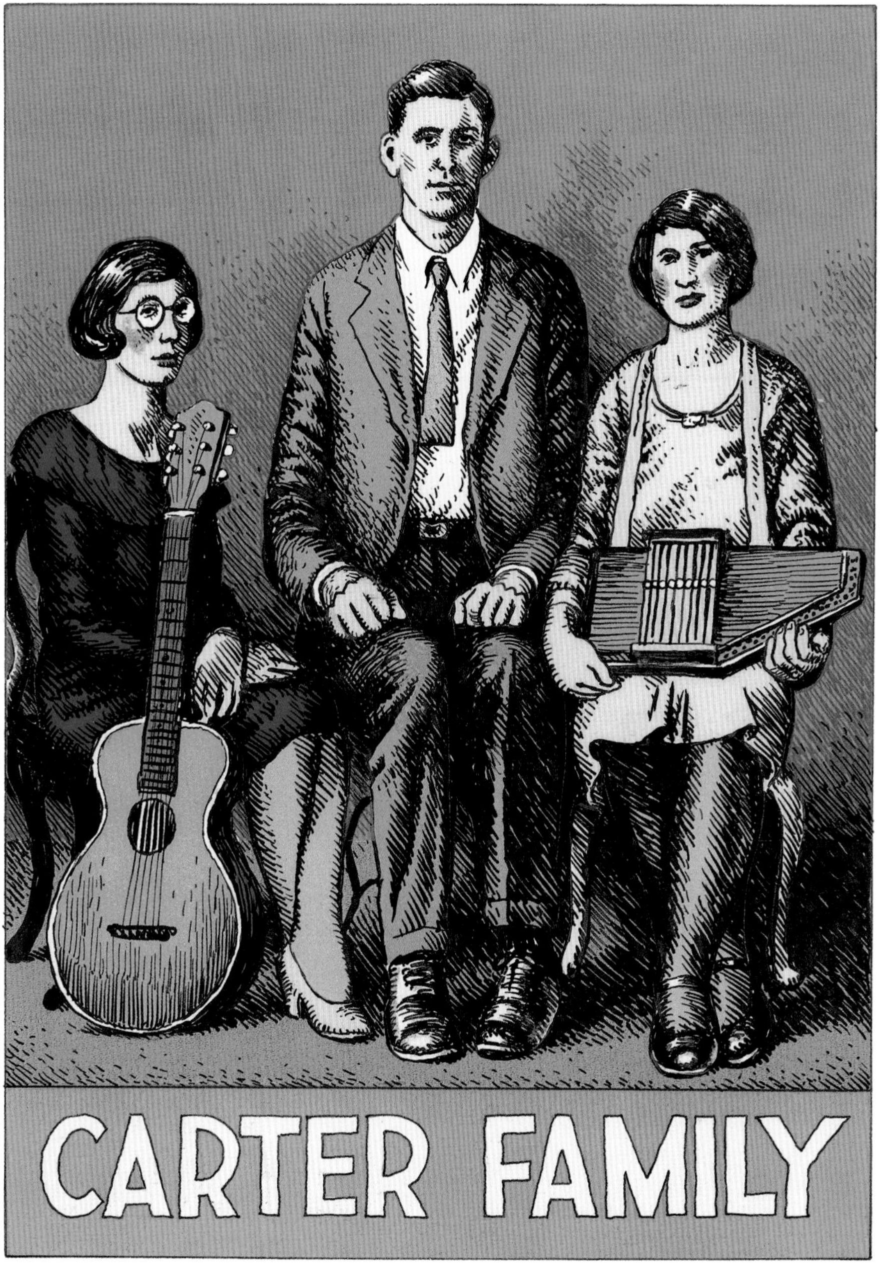
CARTER FAMILY

# FIDDLIN' DOC ROBERTS TRIO

| **Doc Roberts** | **Ted Chesnut** | **Dick Parman** |
|---|---|---|
| FIDDLE | MANDOLIN | GUITAR |
| B: *Madison County, Kentucky, April 26, 1897* | B: *Unknown* | B: *Unknown* |
| D: *August 4, 1978* | D: *Unknown* | D: *Unknown* |

Born in 1897 in Madison County, Kentucky, Dock Philip "Doc" Roberts was one of the finest fiddlers recorded in the 1920s and 1930s. During his ten-year recording career with Gennett Records, American Recording Company, and Paramount Records, Roberts recorded more than eighty outstanding traditional tunes, almost all of which were fine examples of the repertoire of his native Kentucky. He was one of the more technically proficient fiddlers of the period, had a wonderfully rich tone, and captured perfectly all the subtle cadences and sweet bluesy accents of the central Kentucky style he represented. Roberts's main stylistic influence was Owen Walker, a renowned elderly black fiddler who was born in 1857 and from whom Roberts got most of his tunes. African Americans in Kentucky seem to have had a much more profound impact on the usually white domain of fiddle music (which was predominantly Celtic in origin), and Roberts's music, along with that of black Kentucky fiddler Jim Booker, represents the only remaining links to this fascinating chapter in American music history. Although a different band is pictured in this illustration, Roberts's most frequent recording partner was Asa Martin, who backed him on guitar, and who in later sessions was joined by Roberts's son James. Only the remarkable body of fiddle tunes recorded by Clark Kessinger, perhaps the finest fiddler of the whole period, compares with Roberts's work in size and scope.

**FIDDLIN' DOC ROBERTS TRIO**

# TED GOSSETT OF
# TED GOSSETT'S STRING BAND

**FIDDLE**

*B: Near Graham, Kentucky, 1904*
*D: Unknown*

The recordings made by Ted Gossett's band are totally unique in style. The fiddling, whether on the six selections featuring Ted Gossett or the three featuring Tommy Whitmer, is highlighted by explosive dynamics and clipped, abrupt phrasing. The guitar backup is unusual, often stressing off-beats with bass runs that are only loosely related to the melody. The staccato finger-picked banjo playing, like the fiddle, has a frenzied propulsion, and the overall ensemble effect is exciting and wild. Gossett was born in 1904 near Graham, Kentucky, and learned the rudiments of fiddling from his father, Noah "Big Son" Gossett. Whitmer, who sounds almost exactly like Gossett, was a full generation older, having been born in 1886 near Bremen, Kentucky. Both were mighty fiddlers with great drive and rich tone. All the members of the band were from Muhlenberg County, Kentucky. The guitarists were Earl Nossinger and Enos Gossett; Pete Woods played banjo. The band's nine selections were recorded for Gennett in 1930. Today their music stands as some of the most exciting country string-band music ever recorded.

**TED GOSSETT** of
**TED GOSSETT'S STRING BAND**

# JIMMIE RODGERS

**GUITAR**

B: *Meridian, Mississippi, September 8, 1897*
D: *New York, New York, May 26, 1933*

Of all the thousands of rural performers who recorded in the 1920s, none had more impact on the American music scene than Jimmie Rodgers. His influence was profound: it can be said that he alone was responsible for the development of all country and western music that followed. In the ensuing fifteen to twenty years, every important country performer was overwhelmingly influenced by Rodgers. His repertoire came from all corners of American music, drawing heavily on smooth uptown blues and sentimental Tin Pan Alley favorites. Many of the compositions Rodgers recorded (most of which were self-penned or composed by his sister-in-law, Elsie McWilliams) were in these genres.

The inclination to write new songs that incorporated the older sounds but spoke directly to contemporary interests was at the heart of the development of commercial country music. Rodgers's style paralleled this pattern: he had all the feel of the older rural performers, but was also sophisticated and contemporary in his delivery and arrangements. Born in Meridian, Mississippi, in 1897, he died an untimely, tragic death from tuberculosis in 1933, one day after his last recording session. All of Rodgers's extensive recorded repertoire was made for Victor Records between 1927 and 1933. During that period, his recordings sold more total copies than any other performer in the industry.

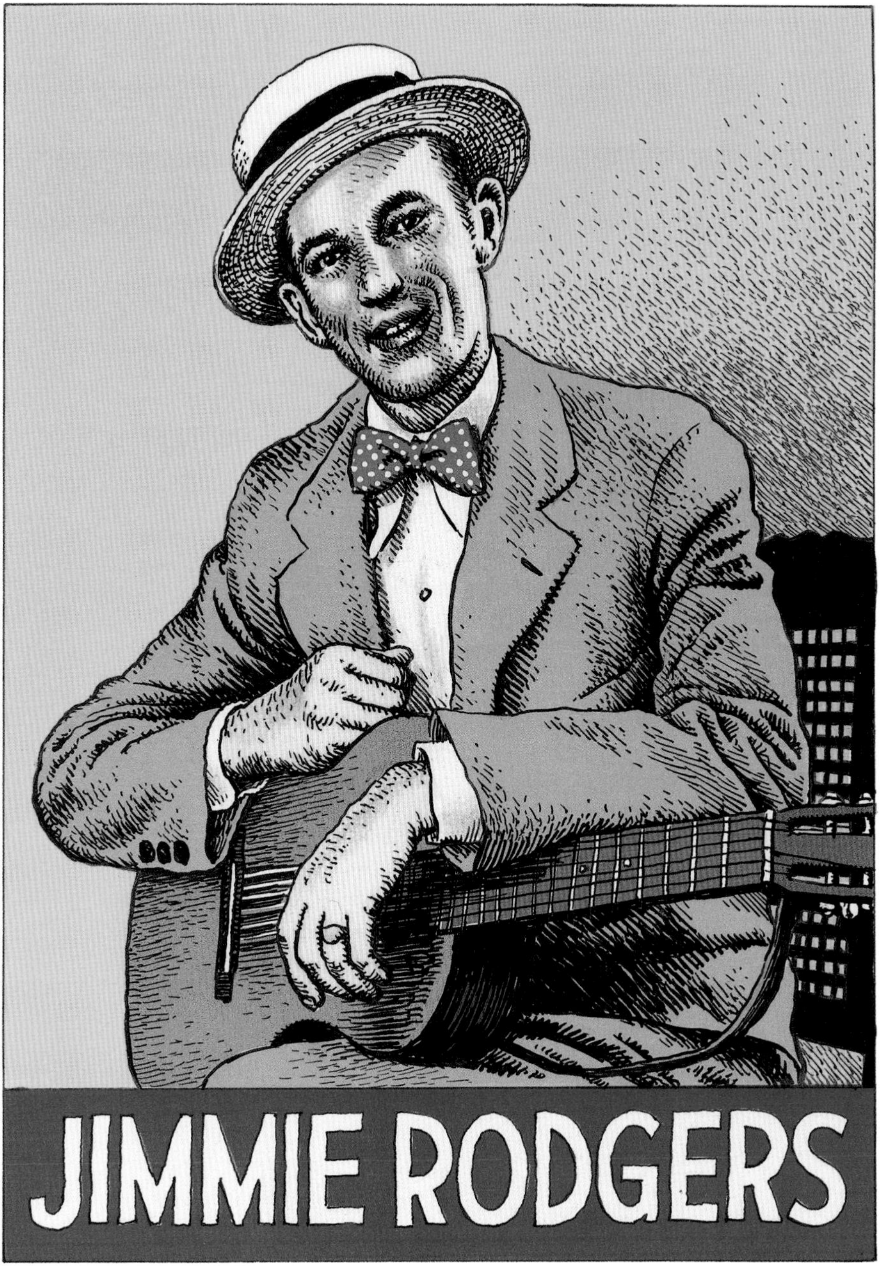
JIMMIE RODGERS

# HARRY "MAC" McCLINTOCK

**VOCALS**

B: *Knoxville, Tennessee, October 8, 1882*
D: *San Francisco, California, April 24, 1957*

Harry "Haywire Mac" McClintock was born in Knoxville, Tennessee, in 1882 and led a fascinatingly diverse life before settling into the role of a cowboy singer. He was at various times a mule skinner, a railroad man, a union organizer, a medicine-show entertainer, a steamboat performer, and at the tender age of fourteen, when he left home for good, he was a member of the Gentry Brothers Dog and Pony Show. McClintock became a cowboy singer because he found enthusiastic acceptance for cowboy songs at the mining camps and cowtowns into which he drifted. Landing steady work on radio in 1925 solidified his newfound career. The repertoire he sang was easy to acquire, as it was common both orally and in print. Most cowboy singers sang the same songs, many of which were first printed as poems in western papers in the 1870s and 1880s. McClintock recorded more than twenty selections for Victor Records in the late 1920s, and four for Decca Records in the 1930s. With the exception of Dick Devall, who sang with a somber modality that more accurately portrayed the real drudgery of the Old West, all the cowboy singers of the 1920s and 1930s were caught up in an unbelievably romanticized image of western life. It was an image promulgated and cultivated by what was then the mass media of print — an image that was to have remarkable impact on the American psyche from that time on.

# HARRY "MAC" McCLINTOCK

# DR. HUMPHREY BATE AND HIS POSSUM HUNTERS

| **Dr. Humphrey Bate** | **Stalry Walton** | **James Hart** |
|---|---|---|
| HARMONICA | GUITAR | GUITAR |
| B: *Castillian Springs,* | B: *Unknown* | B: *Unknown* |
| *Tennessee, May 25, 1875* | D: *Unknown* | D: *Unknown* |
| D: *June 12, 1936* | | |

| **Bill Barret** | **Walter Ligget** | **Oscar Albright** |
|---|---|---|
| FIDDLE | BANJO | DOUBLE BASS |
| B: *Unknown* | B: *Unknown* | B: *Unknown* |
| D: *Unknown* | D: *Unknown* | D: *Unknown* |

Dr. Humphrey Bate, the genial country physician from Castillian Springs, Tennessee, was the founder and leader of the Possum Hunters. His band was the first and one of the most popular to appear on the early Grand Ole Opry. A first-rate harmonica player himself, his musically strong group included Stalry Walton and James Hart, guitars; Oscar Stone and Bill Barret, fiddles; Walter Ligget, banjo; and Oscar Albright, double bass. Stylistically, their music was firmly rooted in western Tennessee. Featuring the dramatic contrast between a smooth, flowing bowed bass and a Morse Code–sounding banjo, the Possum Hunters sound was very similar to Weems String Band (see page 228), another classic group from the same general area. Bate was middle-aged in 1928, when he recorded for Brunswick/ Vocalion. The band reflected this and played an older style of traditional music. The staccato brilliance of these sixteen titles documents a major branch of early American music. Bate and his group played very actively on radio and in public until his death in 1936.

DR. HUMPHREY BATE
AND HIS POSSUM HUNTERS

# UNCLE DAVE MACON AND HIS FRUIT-JAR DRINKERS

| **Uncle Dave Macon** | **Sam McGee** | **Kirk McGee** | **Mazy Todd** |
|---|---|---|---|
| BANJO | GUITAR | VOCALS, FIDDLE | FIDDLE |
| B: *Smart Station, Warren County, Tennessee, October 7, 1870*<br>D: *March 22, 1952* | B: *Unknown*<br>D: *Unknown* | B: *Unknown*<br>D: *Unknown* | B: *Unknown*<br>D: *Unknown* |

Uncle Dave Macon was a giant figure in country music for the first half of the last century and remains so today. While new audiences continue to discover his fine recordings, he is still held in esteem and affection by the multitudes of people who listened to him during the twenty–five years when he was a mainstay at the Grand Ole Opry. Born in 1870 in Smart Station, Warren County, Tennessee, Macon learned much of his varied banjo tech-niques and amazingly broad repertoire both from traditional sources in the Tennessee countryside and from the stream of minstrel and vaudeville musicians who frequented his family's hotel, which they maintained after moving to Nashville. Macon's singing and rollicking banjo playing were rather unpolished, but were inspiring in their joyful vitality and boundless energy. His finest recordings were made in 1926 and 1927 for Vocalion Records, with the assistance of fellow Tennesseans Sam McGee (one of the truly great country guitar players of the period); Kirk McGee, a fine singer and fiddler; and Mazy Todd, an excellent traditional fiddler. Collectively they were known as the Fruit–Jar Drinkers. Macon made hundreds of recordings from 1924 to 1938, predominantly for Brunswick/Vocalion, but also for Okeh Records, Gennett Records, and Bluebird Records. He died in 1952, leaving a legacy of countless enduring classic recordings, many of which are the only documentations of a priceless body of American songs.

# UNCLE DAVE MACON
## AND HIS FRUIT-JAR DRINKERS

# BURNETT & RUTHERFORD

### Dick Burnett

**GUITAR, BANJO, VOCALS**

B: *Vicinity of Monticello, Kentucky, 1883*

D: *1977*

### Leonard Rutherford

**FIDDLE, VOCALS**

B: *Vicinity of Monticello, Kentucky, c. 1900*

D: *1954*

Burnett & Rutherford, from the Monticello, Kentucky, area, was musically one of the premier country groups to record in the 1920s. Leonard Rutherford's smooth-as-silk fiddling contrasted starkly with Dick Burnett's dramatically punctuated staccato rhythms on both guitar and banjo. This possibly troublesome juxtaposition actually worked in their favor, imbuing their music with eloquent finesse and raw backcountry power. Adding greatly to the quality of their performances was the extremely close-knit tightness of Burnett's backups. Rutherford was one of the finest traditional fiddlers ever recorded. He had the loosest bow-hand wrist action of any fiddler, and could change bow direction effortlessly. This rare talent accounts for his amazing smoothness and exquisite tone. Rutherford's technique was altogether unique. Others would have played like him if they could have, but his bowing was far too demanding. Like their instrumentals, Rutherford's vocals were smoother while Burnett's were coarser. Burnett was born in 1883. He turned professionally to music in 1907 after being blinded by a gunshot wound to the face. Rutherford was almost fourteen when, in 1914, Burnett took him under his wing. For the next thirty-five years they constantly traveled and played music throughout the South. They recorded extensively for Columbia Records and Gennett Records from 1926 to 1930, and left a legacy of many of the finest performances of the period.

BURNETT & RUTHERFORD

# MUMFORD BEAN AND HIS ITAWAMBIANS

| **Mumford Bean** | **Relder Priddy** | **Morine Little** |
|:---:|:---:|:---:|
| FIDDLE | MANDOLIN | GUITAR |
| B: c. 1916 | B: Unknown | B: Unknown |
| D: Unknown | D: Unknown | D: Unknown |

The sole released record of Mumford Bean features two old-time waltzes. Bean was only twelve when he recorded these tunes for Okeh Records in 1928. His fiddling was augmented by relatives Relder Priddy on mandolin and Morine Little on guitar. The band was from Itawamba County in northeast Mississippi. Being inescapably surrounded by music since birth, and aided by traditional open tunings that demanded little fretting, many rural musicians started playing at an early age. The fact that numerous family members were also musicians helped the early starter in the availability of firsthand teachers and the proximity of already-tuned instruments on which to practice.

**MUMFORD BEAN**
AND HIS ITAWAMBIANS

# SHELOR FAMILY

**Joe "Dad" Blackard**
BANJO, VOCALS

**Clarice Shelor**
PIANO, VOCALS

**Jesse Shelor**
FIDDLE

**Pyrus Shelor**
FIDDLE

The Shelor Family from Patrick County, Virginia (also known as Dad Blackard's Moonshiners), consisted of Joe "Dad" Blackard on banjo and vocals; his daughter, Clarice Shelor, on piano and vocals; her husband, Jesse, on fiddle; and his brother, Pyrus, also on fiddle. They recorded four brilliant sides for Victor Records in 1927, and like most country artists of the period, returned the next day to total anonymity, never to record again. More than ninety percent of the early rural bands that recorded were composed of members in their twenties or younger. This is still true of pop bands today and probably in most eras. These young rural musicians viewed themselves as "pop" performers. Although they were playing well-worn selections, their performances and interpretations were structured to please the current tastes of their own time and place. Older musicians rarely got to record, but when they did their recordings offered a rare view into the music of the mid-1800s. Blackard, born before the Civil War, contributes just such a component to the Shelor's music both in his sedate but jaunty gait and his addition to the group's repertoire of otherwise obscure gems like "Big Bend Gal." In fact, Blackard gave a number of fine old ballads to noted musical historian Cecil Sharp in 1918.

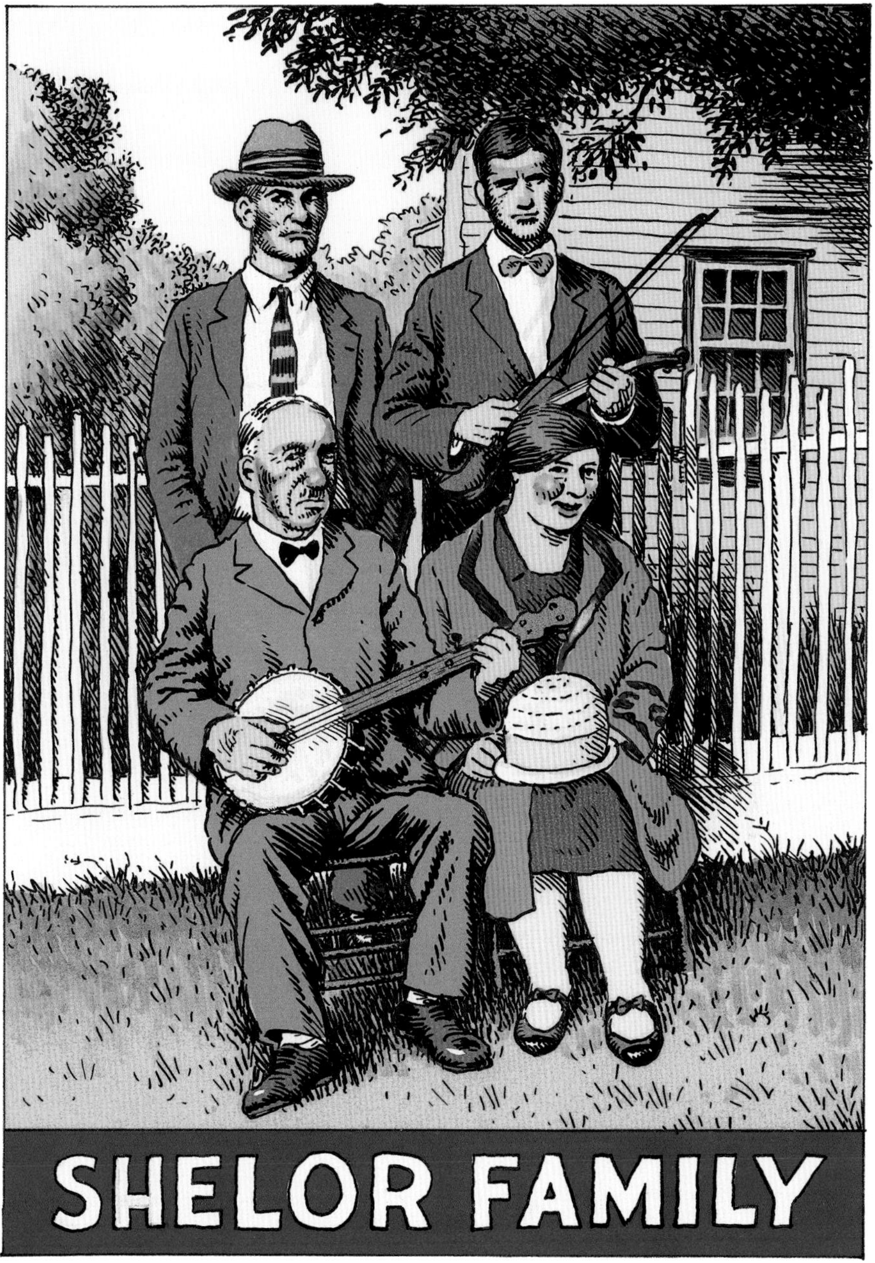
SHELOR FAMILY

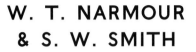

# W. T. NARMOUR
# & S. W. SMITH

**Will (W. T.) Narmour**

FIDDLE

B: *1889*

D: *Unknown*

**Shell (S. W.) Smith**

GUITAR

B: *1895*

D: *Unknown*

The fiddle-guitar duets of Narmour & Smith are immediately identifiable as Mississippi music. In the more mountainous Appalachian areas of the South, fiddlers animated their bowing with quick back-and-forth figures of very short notes that conveyed a highly syncopated rhythm. They were dance oriented and tuned their strings high above standard pitch, preferring the keys of A and D. Conversely, Mississippi fiddlers tended to tune well below concert pitch, favoring the keys of C and G, which added a warm, mellow feel, but diminished the dance appeal. In contrast to the Appalachian bowing, Mississippi fiddlers opted for full, rich tone and sweet, prolonged sculpting of notes and phrases, leaving the rhythm to the backup, which was less syncopated than its other southern counterparts. Will (W. T.) Narmour was a good example of a Mississippi fiddler, squeezing every nuance of expression out of each note. Shell (S. W.) Smith was a rudimentary guitar player who often ignored the necessary chord changes, but did an outstanding job of supporting Narmour's fiddle. Their odd hitches of rhythm and bluesy intonations give Narmour & Smith a distinctive sound within the Mississippi mold they fit so well. They recorded thirty-one songs for Okeh Records in the late 1920s and repeated many of them for Bluebird Records in the 1930s.

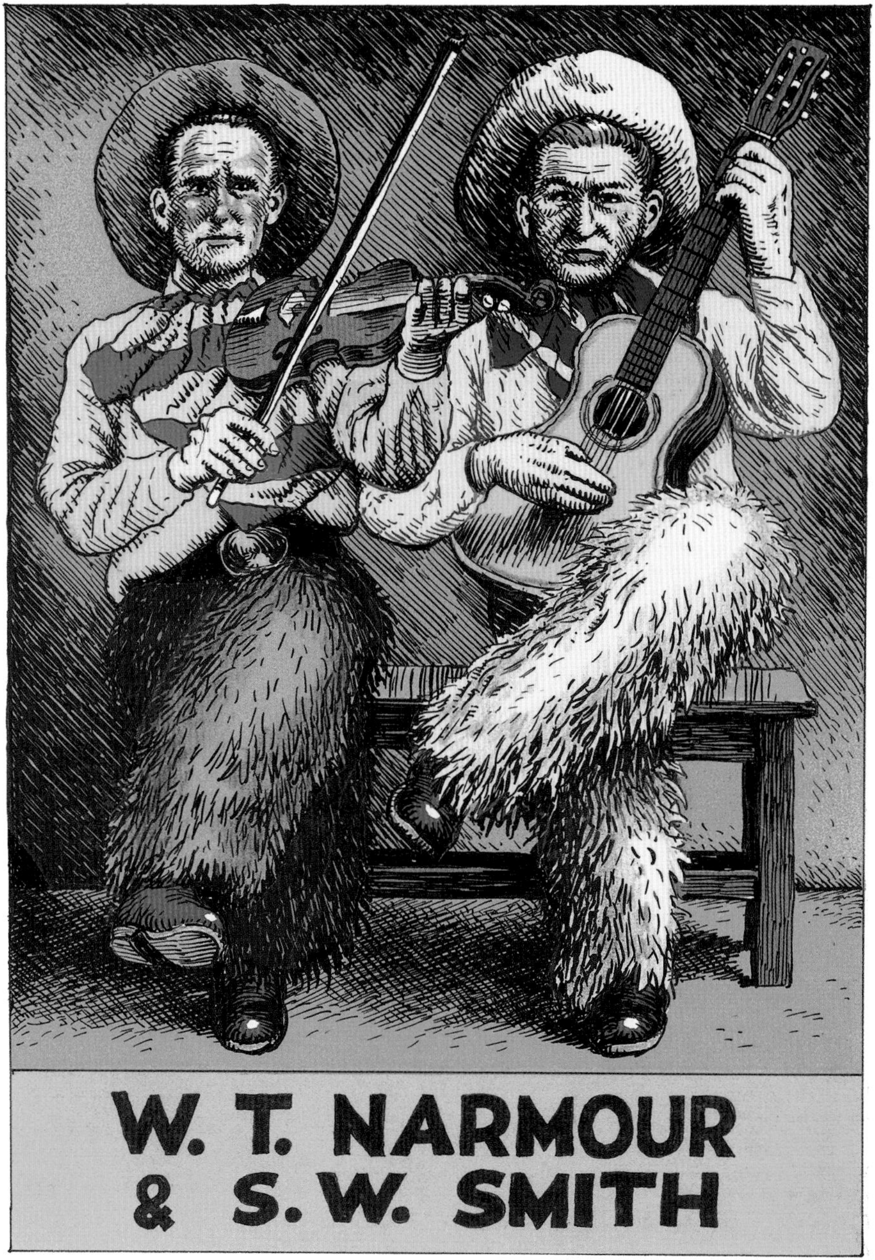

**W. T. NARMOUR & S. W. SMITH**

# RAY BROTHERS

**Will Ray**
GUITAR
B: *Choctaw County, Chester, Mississippi*
D: *Unknown*

**Vardeman Ray**
FIDDLE
B: *Choctaw County, Chester, Mississippi*
D: *Unknown*

It seems likely that early settlers coming to America from the British Isles brought at least six or seven distinct and separate traditions of fiddle music. For example, the fiddle styles of Alabama and Mississippi are unique in their full, rich body and tone and their gliding rhythm, and seem almost unrelated to their more insistent counterparts played throughout most of the South. A perfect example of this sweet, engaging style is the music of the Ray Brothers from the Choctaw County town of Chester, Mississippi. Will Ray and his brother, Vardeman (playing guitar and fiddle, respectively, shown here with three brothers), formed one of the finest fiddle–guitar ensembles ever recorded, rivaled only by the Stripling Brothers, their

Alabama twins. The mellowness of the fiddle styles throughout Alabama and Mississippi was augmented by the common practice of tuning the fiddle well below concert pitch. This tradition is in marked contrast to most of the South, where the fiddle is tuned well above concert pitch to help carry the sound at dances. Because of more bass melody notes and sophisticated use of passing chords, the finger-picked guitar accompaniment was more complex in these two states than the rudimentary "boom chang" style that was common in most of the South. The ten tunes recorded for Victor Records in 1930, which represent the whole output of the Ray Brothers, are lauded for demonstrating musicianship of the highest standard.

RAY BROTHERS

# THE TENNESSEE RAMBLERS

| **Bill Sievers** | **Mack Sievers** | **Willie Sievers** | **Walt McKinney** |
|---|---|---|---|
| FIDDLE | BANJO | GUITAR | GUITAR |
| B: Knoxville, | B: Knoxville, | B: Knoxville, | B: Knoxville, |
| Tennessee, area, 1875 | Tennessee, area | Tennessee, area | Tennessee, area |
| D: Unknown | D: Unknown | D: Unknown | D: Unknown |

The Tennessee Ramblers was a family group from the Knoxville area whose members were Bill Sievers (born in 1875) on fiddle; his son, Mack, and daughter, Willie, on banjo and guitar, respectively; and their cousin, Walt McKinney, on steel guitar. They recorded eleven songs released on the Brunswick/Vocalion labels in the late 1920s. Stylistically, the band sounded like the groups of Earl Johnson (see page 170), a family friend. The band even recorded some of the same material as Johnson. Although musically adequate, much of the band's popularity rested on its ability to entertain. The Ramblers had an "entertainment first" policy, and this is reflected in the humorous content and cutup performances of the group's records.

THE TENNESSEE RAMBLERS

# ERNEST STONEMAN AND
# THE BLUE RIDGE CORN SHUCKERS

| **Ernest Stoneman** | **Iver Edwards** | **George Stoneman** |
|---|---|---|
| GUITAR, VOCALS | UKULELE | BANJO |
| B: *Monarat (Iron Ridge),* | B: *Unknown* | B: *Unknown* |
| *Virginia, May 25, 1893* | D: *Unknown* | D: *Unknown* |
| D: *June 14, 1968* | | |

| **Eck Dunford** | **Hattie Stoneman** | **Bolen Frost** |
|---|---|---|
| FIDDLE | FIDDLE | BANJO |
| B: *Unknown* | B: *Unknown* | B: *Unknown* |
| D: *Unknown* | D: *Unknown* | D: *Unknown* |

Ernest Stoneman's greatest contribution to early country music was not so much as an artist, but as an unwitting talent scout. The amazing, ever-changing roster of performers he brought to the studio to record accounted for quite a legacy of great music. A partial list includes Eck Dunford, Frank and Oscar Jenkins, The Sweet Brothers, Kahle Brewer, Emmett Lundy, Fields Ward, Irma Frost, and Hattie Stoneman. These fine artists, together with Stoneman's own good instincts for arrangements, were responsible for the high level of musicianship on his recordings. Stoneman was immersed in music from childhood. When early country 78s first appeared, he contacted the major recording companies and soon was recording extensively to his own autoharp and harmonica accompaniment for the Okeh Records label. His acoustically recorded (pre-1926) efforts are very weak musically, as were the majority of all country records in the 1923–26 period. With the advent of electric recording and the utilization of a full band format, Stoneman's records improved considerably and many became genre classics. Stylistically, all the various Stoneman groups share characteristics of spare, unembellished melody lines, a loose, easy gait, and picture-perfect phrasing. Stoneman recorded more than two hundred songs, fiddle tunes, sacred numbers, and skits for Victor Records, Okeh Records, Gennett Records, Edison Records, and the American Record Company. Pop Stoneman, as he was known to all in later years, died in 1968.

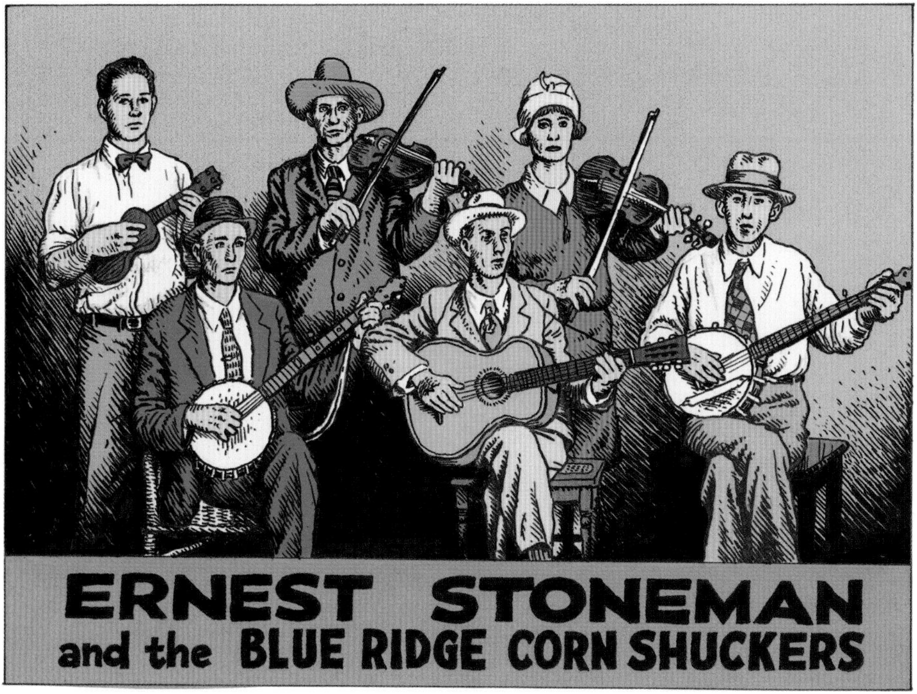
ERNEST STONEMAN
and the BLUE RIDGE CORN SHUCKERS

# SHEPHERD BROTHERS

### Bill Shepherd
**VOCALS, FIDDLE**
B: *Jenkins, Kentucky*
D: *Unknown*

### Hayes Shepherd
**BANJO**
B: *Jenkins, Kentucky*
D: *Unknown*

Unique styles flourished around the Kentucky-Virginia border in the 1920s. This area generated music known for its machine-gun phrasing, high-pitched vocal projection, and blues-tinged structure. Among the region's finest were Bill and Hayes Shepherd from Jenkins, Kentucky. Their playing was similar to that of "Dock" Boggs (see page 222) of West Norton, Virginia, but was performed with more force and drive. The Shepherds were representative of eastern Kentucky both in their use of Bill's high-tenor falsetto singing and the sacred-blues style that shaped all their performances. Melodically, many blues bear a notable resemblance to early white-fundamentalist religious music. The limited scales are almost identical and they share a common modality. If the speed of an archaic primitive Baptist hymn is doubled, the striking similarity to blues is apparent.

Of Bill Shepherd's ten recorded songs (for Gennett Records in 1932), only two were issued. They are both masterpieces that were stylistic precursors of Bill Monroe's best recordings made fifteen to twenty years later, and highlight the same high, plaintive vocal sound that has so frequently been associated with Kentucky. These recordings feature Hayes and another brother on banjos and Ed Webb on guitar. Hayes's strident singing and banjo playing were featured on his only solo effort, which was recorded by Vocalion in 1930 and produced two of the best performances of the era. The tragic loss of eight unissued Gennett Shepherd songs sadly reflects that company's prejudice toward generations-old traditional vocals. A phrase that should live in infamy appears all too often in the Gennett ledgers: "Rejected—too much backwoods."

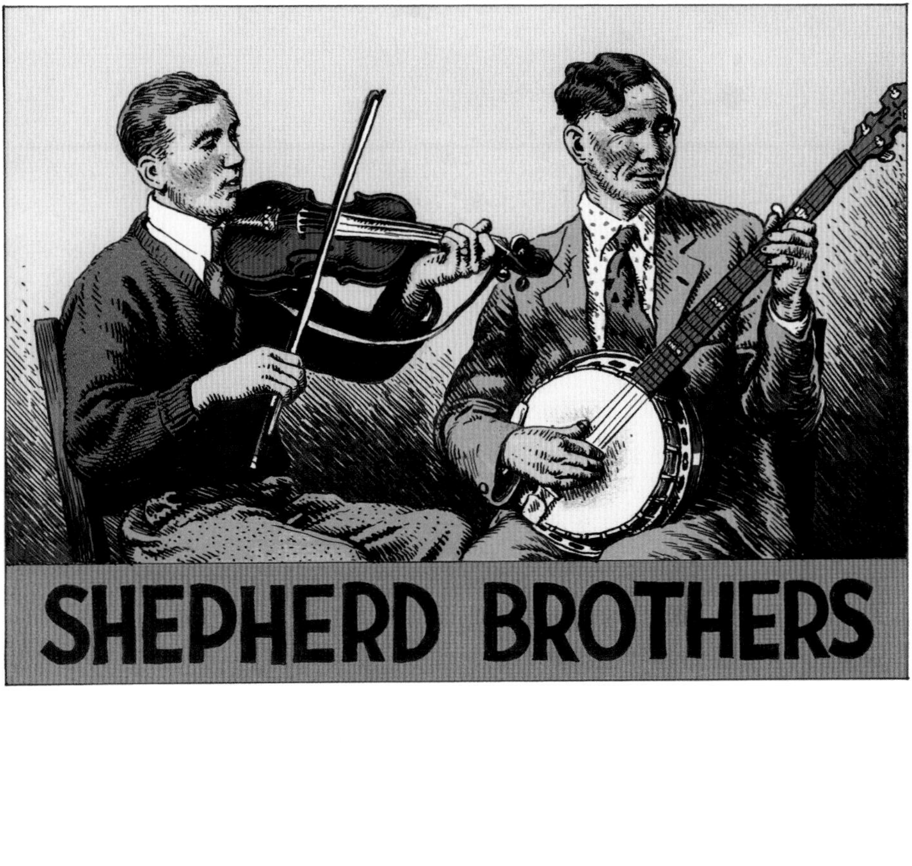
SHEPHERD BROTHERS

# TAYLOR-GRIGGS
# LOUISIANA MELODY MAKERS

| **Foster Taylor** | **Robert Grigg** | **Ausie Grigg** |
|:---:|:---:|:---:|
| FIDDLE | FIDDLE, VOCALS | DOUBLE BASS |

| **Lorean Grigg** | **Ione Grigg** | **Crockett Grigg** | **Clavie Taylor** |
|:---:|:---:|:---:|:---:|
| MANDOLIN | GUITAR | VOCALS | VOCALS |

The music of Taylor–Griggs Louisiana Melody Makers from near Arcadia, Louisiana, was distinctive. It was by far the mellowest and smoothest of any old–time band that recorded. These characteristics, which are representative of deep southern stylings, were heightened by a choice of material that featured predominantly slow vocals and waltzes. The beautiful bowed double bass playing of Ausie Grigg added to this effect. The four selections made at their first recording session (the band shown here) featured either Foster Taylor or Robert Grigg (Ausie's father) on fiddle, Ausie on double bass, and his sisters Lorean on mandolin and Ione on guitar. Vocals were sung by brother Crockett, Robert, and Clavie Taylor (a nephew of Foster's). The second Victor Records session, at which six selections were recorded, featured Foster, Ausie, Bun Hiser on mandolin, Henry Galloway on guitar, and Oscar Logan on vocals. All ten of these recordings have a quality that makes them seem suspended in time, and as such convey perfectly the laconic grace of deep southern life.

TAYLOR-GRIGGS LOUISIANA MELODY MAKERS

# JIMMIE & GEORGE CARTER OF CARTER BROTHERS & SON

**Jimmie Carter**
GUITAR
B: *Near Harley, northeast Mississippi*
D: *Unknown*

**George Carter**
FIDDLE, VOCALS
B: *Near Harley, northeast Mississippi, 1874*
D: *Unknown*

Of all the hundreds of early country groups that recorded in the 1920s and 1930s, none has intrigued enthusiasts more than Carter Brothers & Son. The band had an unbridled exuberance and a wild, reckless self-abandon that evoked an image of American music in its earliest, least intellectualized form. George (born 1874) and Andrew (born 1878) Carter were in their fifties when the group's ten selections were recorded for Okeh Records and Vocalion in 1928, and their fiddling represents a much older style than most of the period. It is fascinating to realize that well over ninety percent of the musicians recording traditional music in the 1920s were in their twenties or younger; this was the pop music of its time and place. Rounding out the band was George's son, Jimmie, an outstanding guitar player. George played lead fiddle and Andy seconded, alternating between a baritone harmony and unison melody. Their explosive dynamics, together with George's frenzied, often incoherent vocals, created a whirlwind of musical excitement. On one of their finest recordings, "Give the Fiddler a Dram," they get so caught up in the headfirst propulsion of the music that George and Andy find themselves playing two different parts of the tune, but it still comes out as great music! The Carters were from near Harley in northeast Mississippi, but their style has little relation to most Mississippi music, sounding more like the duet fiddling of neighboring Arkansas. In the months when they were not cotton farming, the Carters were professional musicians on riverboats plying the Mississippi.

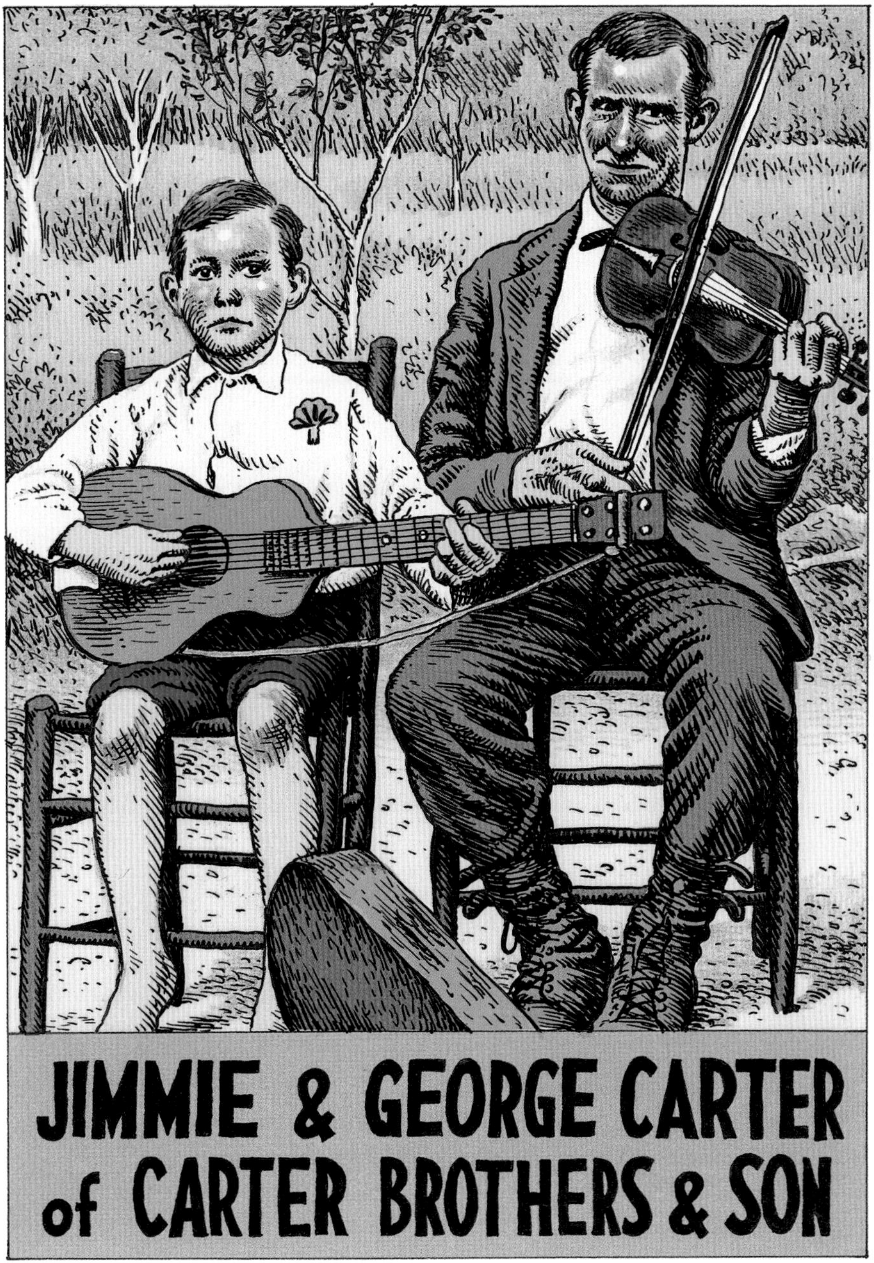

JIMMIE & GEORGE CARTER
of CARTER BROTHERS & SON

# HOYT MING AND HIS PEP STEPPERS

| Hoyt Ming | Roselle Ming | Troy Ming | A. D. Coggin |
|---|---|---|---|
| FIDDLE, VOCALS | GUITAR | MANDOLIN | VOCALS |
| B: 1902 | B: Unknown | B: Unknown | B: Unknown |
| D: Unknown | D: Unknown | D: Unknown | D: Unknown |

Hoyt Ming's Pep Steppers was one of the most unusual bands of the whole early era of recording. Their unique sound was the product of sweet, smooth Mississippi fiddling, taken to its furthest limits of laid-back mellowness, and a tightly knit rhythm section highlighted by foot tapping. Ming employed many accentuated slides and slurs in his distinctive fiddling, which was so drawn out as to sound at times like a slowly extended accordion. Hoyt's wife, Roselle, provided the especially strident guitar backup and footwork, and his brother, Troy, played the mandolin. Also at the session—during which four tunes were recorded for Victor Records—was A. D. Coggin, who added charming dance calls that fit the music perfectly. The group, which was from the Tupelo area, recorded only once, and returned the next day to their usual work-a-day lifestyles and total anonymity. More than ninety percent of the rural musicians recorded in this early period fit this pattern of short one-shot sessions, during which only four to six selections were recorded in makeshift field studios. Not surprisingly, such sessions produced the majority of enduring classics such as those of Ming's Pep Steppers. The band's musical trademark was "Indian War Whoop," in which Ming added vocal whoops to the eerie harmonics of the fiddle melody.

# HOYT MING
## AND HIS PEP STEPPERS

# PAUL MILES AND
# HIS RED FOX CHASERS

| Paul Miles | A. P. Thompson | Bob Cranford | Guy Brooks |
|------------|----------------|--------------|------------|
| BANJO | GUITAR, VOCALS | MOUTH HARP, VOCALS | FIDDLE |

The sound of the Red Fox Chasers was built around the harmony singing of A. P. Thompson and Bob Cranford, who had sung together since childhood in Surry County, North Carolina. As teenagers, Thompson became proficient on guitar and Cranford, on mouth harp. They began to entertain locally on a semiprofessional basis. The Red Fox Chasers was formed in 1927 when Thompson and Cranford were joined by fiddler Guy Brooks and banjoist Paul Miles, both of whom also occasionally sang vocals. The band recorded forty-eight sides for Gennett Records that were, as was common for that company, issued on a variety of mail-order labels under many pseudonyms like the Virginia Possum Tamers. The Red Fox Chasers' renditions of many sentimental ballads of earlier Tin Pan Alley origin display perfectly the rural artist's ability to transpose such soppy tearjerkers and impart a treatment tempered by traditional Appalachian attitudes toward instrumentation and vocal delivery.

PAUL MILES and his RED FOX CHASERS

# ROANE COUNTY RAMBLERS

**Jimmy McCarroll**
FIDDLE

**Luke Brandon**
GUITAR

**John Kelly**
MANDOLIN

**Howard Wyatt**
BANJO

The Roane County Ramblers from East Tennessee consisted of Jimmy McCarroll on fiddle, Luke Brandon on guitar, John Kelly on mandolin, and Howard Wyatt on banjo. They issued twelve tunes on Columbia Records in 1928–29, all of which are characterized by extremely tight-knit ensemble playing, boundless exuberance, and the brilliant, blazing fiddling of McCarroll. Stylistically, the Ramblers' sound was quite similar to that of north Georgia groups, especially Earl Johnson's (see page 170). McCarroll employed the same kind of exaggerated slides as Johnson and a similarly unrelenting propulsion, but was technically far superior. Like the Skillet Lickers of north Georgia, the Roane County Ramblers were attempting to be progressive, appealing to contemporary tastes with sophisticated settings and flashy technique. Juxtaposing this aesthetic on some of the more archaic pieces in their repertoire made for unusual transformations, as when the classic old fiddle tune "Last of the Callahan" became "Callahan Rag."

**ROANE COUNTY RAMBLERS**

# FRANK BLEVINS AND HIS TAR HEEL RATTLERS

**Frank Blevins**
FIDDLE, VOCALS
B: *Alleghany County,
North Carolina*
D: *Unknown*

**Fred Miller**
BANJO, VOCALS
B: *Unknown*
D: *Unknown*

**Ed Blevins**
GUITAR, VOCALS
B: *Unknown*
D: *Unknown*

**Jack Reedy**
BANJO
B: *Unknown*
D: *Unknown*

Within the seemingly simple context of very rudimentary melodies played with a stark minimum of embellishment, backcountry musicians like Frank Blevins and His Tar Heel Rattlers made music of rare eloquence. Like so many other great early rural bands, the Tar Heel Rattlers had great expressiveness in their performances and wove considerable warmth into their music. These qualities are central to old-time traditional music, and in the final analysis are impressive and far more difficult to reproduce than any technical wizardry. Blevins, from Alleghany County, North Carolina, was only fifteen years old at the time of the group's sessions (eight issued selections for Columbia Records), which he alone

organized. He played fiddle and sang most of the vocals, Fred Miller played banjo and sang two vocals, and Blevins's brother, Ed, played guitar and sang two vocals. Ed Blevins's guitar playing is worthy of special attention both for the important role it played within the band, and because it was typical of the period. Early rural guitar players like Ed Blevins used a thumb pick on the bass strings to make accentuated notes that closely completed the fiddler at key points in both the melody and rhythm. The full, rich, sustained tonality of the bass notes acted like a drone, reinforcing the mood of these old rural performances. In many early classic recordings, the guitar plays as important a role as the fiddle itself.

**FRANK BLEVINS**
**AND HIS TAR HEEL RATTLERS**

# CHARLIE POOLE WITH THE NORTH CAROLINA RAMBLERS

| **Charlie Poole** | **Roy Harvey** | **Posey Rorrer** |
|---|---|---|
| BANJO, VOCALS | GUITAR | FIDDLE |
| B: *Spray, North Carolina, March 22, 1892* | B: *West Virginia* | B: *Unknown* |
| D: *May 21, 1931* | D: *Unknown* | D: *Unknown* |

Charlie Poole with the North Carolina Ramblers, one of the most popular and prolific groups in the early years of country music, worked extensively with Columbia Records from 1925 to 1930, and made a few sides for Paramount Records as well. Poole, from Spray, North Carolina, traveled widely, and his records sold extremely well. Much of the Ramblers' success can probably be attributed to the band's laconic, easy-going tempos and smooth, soothing arrangements. At the heart of this style was West Virginian Roy Harvey's brilliant, complex, three-finger guitar playing. In the early sessions Posey Rorrer contributed fine, traditional fiddling; in later sessions Lonnie Austin and Odell Smith added fiddling in a more sophisticated vein. Poole himself sang and played banjo in a three-finger picking style that filled out the band's sound nicely. By the mid-1920s, three-finger banjo styles were coming to the fore as the older staccato techniques lost favor when they conflicted with the evolving smoother rural string band arrangements. The roots of this movement were in eastern Tennessee, where outstanding three-finger players abounded. Poole died in 1931 at the age of only thirty-nine.

CHARLIE POOLE with the
NORTH CAROLINA RAMBLERS

# AL HOPKINS AND
# HIS BUCKLE BUSTERS

**Al Hopkins**

PIANO, VOCALS

B: *Unknown*

D: *Unknown*

**Charlie Bowman**

FIDDLE

B: *Washington County,
Tennessee, 1889*

D: *Unknown*

**Elvis "Tony"
Alderman**

FIDDLE

B: *Unknown*

D: *Unknown*

**Walter Bowman**

BANJO

B: *Unknown*

D: *Unknown*

The Buckle Busters, better known as the Hillbillies, was unusual in that it was a professional touring band that briefly joined a vaudeville circuit and made a short film that was distributed nationally. Their personnel fluctuated widely, especially on records, where specific artists frequently played their specialties only. The core of the group for most of its recordings was Charlie Bowman and Elvis "Tony" Alderman on fiddles; Jack Reedy and Walter Bowman on banjos; Elbert Bowman and Joe Hopkins on guitars; John Hopkins on ukulele; and group leader Al Hopkins on piano and vocals (shown here, second in from the right, playing guitar). At the heart of the band's spirited, up-tempo performances was the brisk, articulate fiddling of Charlie Bowman and the superb, highly developed, melodic, three-finger picking banjo work. Stylistically, the band's sound was an amalgam of the Tennessee styles of the Bowman boys and the Galax, Virginia, genre of Alderman and the Hopkins family. The group recorded prolifically for Brunswick/Vocalion. Their first early acoustic session was made for Okeh Records and featured the outstanding Grayson County, Virginia, clawhammer banjo player John Rector. Simple old-time fiddle tunes, mostly in the "dance" keys of A and D, made up the bulk of the band's repertoire and were always rendered with zest and bounce.

**AL HOPKINS and his BUCKLE BUSTERS**

# FIDDLIN' BOB LARKIN
# AND HIS MUSIC MAKERS

| **Fiddlin' Bob Larkin** | **Forest Larkin** | **Alice Larkin** | **William Holden** |
|---|---|---|---|
| FIDDLE | PIANO | GUITAR | GUITAR |
| B: *New York, New York, 1867* | B: *Unknown* | B: *Unknown* | B: *Unknown* |
| D: *Prairie County, Arkansas* | D: *Unknown* | D: *Unknown* | D: *Unknown* |

Almost all the rural traditional musicians who appeared on early recordings were born and reared in the South. Fiddlin' Bob Larkin is a distinct exception in that not only was he born in the North, but in the heart of New York City. It challenges the imagination to envision a traditional fiddler of such purely backwoods style coming from New York. The catch is that he was born in 1867, when much of the city was predominantly still farmland, and although he learned to fiddle in New York, his stylistic approach may have been shaped more by musicians in Centralia, Missouri, where he moved while still young. After marrying he moved to Prairie County, Arkansas, where he remained for the rest of his life. Larkin was an exciting fiddler whose playing was characterized by bursting dynamics and an uninhibited gusto. He had rich, full tone and an unusual characteristic chirp on his top (E) string. Larkin's great drive was perfectly complemented by his mainly family-derived band. His son Forest played piano; daughter Alice played guitar. William Holden also picked guitar. The group recorded about fourteen selections for Okeh Records and Vocalion in 1928. Fiddlin' Bob Larkin was also a champion marksman, and it was often said that he raised his family of fourteen children with a shotgun and a fiddle. The family played extensively on the radio in Kansas, Texas, and Iowa, most notably for patent medicine mogul Dr. Brinkley.

# FIDDLIN' BOB LARKIN
## AND HIS MUSIC MAKERS

# EAST TEXAS SERENADERS

| Dan "D. H." Williams | Cloet Hamman | Henry Bogan | John Munnerlyn |
|---|---|---|---|
| FIDDLE | GUITAR | CELLO | TENOR BANJO |
| B: Lindale, Texas, 1900 | B: Unknown | B: Unknown | B: Unknown |
| D: Unknown | D: Unknown | D: Unknown | D: Unknown |

The East Texas Serenaders was one of the premier string bands ever recorded. Their repertoire consisted mostly of rags and waltzes, with a few up-tempo selections the band called "stomps." Instrumentation was fiddle, guitar, tenor banjo, and three-string cello. The ensemble rhythm section was superb, as would be expected of a great band. The guitar and banjo provided a driving pulse that propelled the music, and the outstanding bowed cello punctuated the rhythm, sounding like a jug in an old jug band. Dan "D. H." Williams's fiddling was masterful. His smooth, gliding style was typically deep southern, but he also had a brisk, articulate bite to his playing that provided much of the band's exciting dynamics. Williams had a sweet, bluesy touch to his playing, and a rich, mellow tone that was partially the product of vibrato, an unusual technique for a rural fiddler. Lindale, Texas, was Williams's hometown; he was born there in 1900. The group's other members were Cloet Hamman, Henry Bogan, John Munnerlyn, and later Henry and Shorty Lester (it's unclear who the guitarist is on the far left of this illustration). They recorded twenty-four sides for Brunswick, Columbia, and Decca Records from 1927 to 1936.

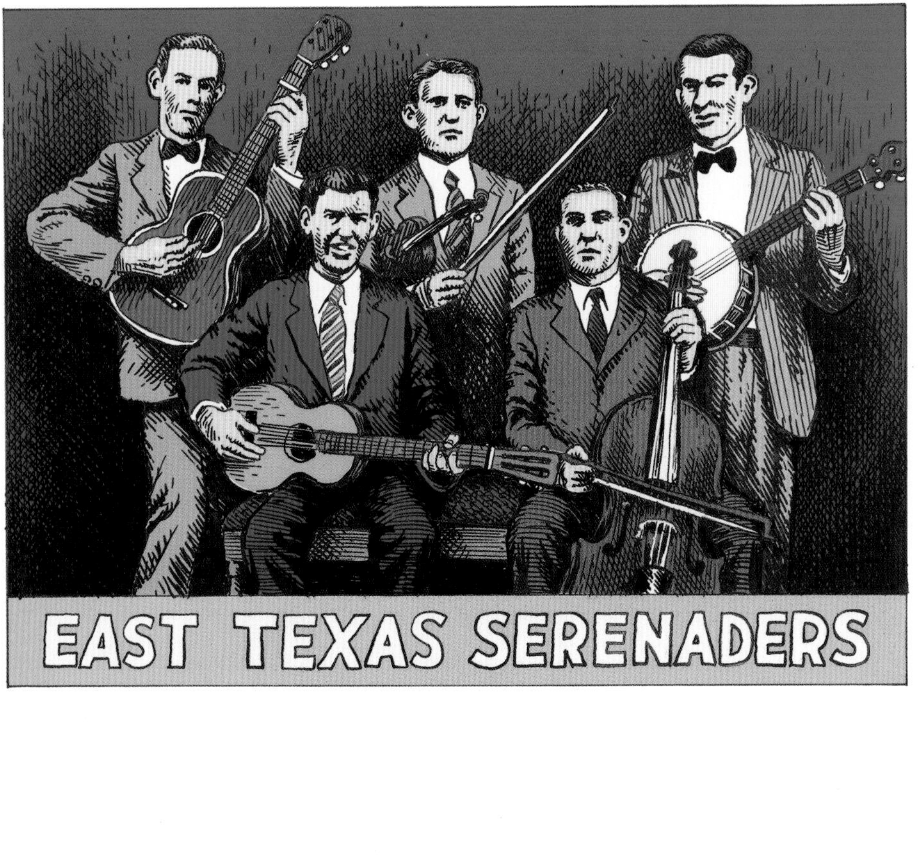
EAST TEXAS SERENADERS

# "DOCK" BOGGS

**BANJO, VOCALS**

*B: West Norton, Virginia, February 7, 1898*
*D: February 7, 1971*

"Dock" Boggs was one of the finest and most distinctive performers to come out of the musically fertile western Virginia/eastern Kentucky area, a locale where coal mining was the economic mainstay. Boggs, born in West Norton, Virginia, in 1898, was also a miner most of his life. His banjo style was rooted in the older picking styles that were prevalent throughout Kentucky, and his music bears a resemblance to the spare but eloquent playing of the great B. F. Shelton from Corbin, Kentucky. Boggs was most individualistic on the banjo, using an eccentric picking pattern of his thumb and first two fingers in a variety of ways. Most commonly he played the lead, which was a semi-melody line, on the first two strings with his index and middle fingers, but on some tunes caught the lead with his thumb on the third and fourth strings. This latter technique produced some of his very best playing. Constantly varying open tunings was also essential to Boggs's playing. Like so many other traditional musicians from earlier eras, he tended to retune for almost every song. When traditional musicians later adopted standard tuning and sophisticated chording, the backups never worked as well as these earlier accompaniments, which seemed to act like a second voice complementing the vocals. Boggs's singing was endemic to Kentucky, maintaining a high-pitched, plaintive intensity, and embodying very bluesy nuances that were of both white and black, common and overlapping origin. Most of Boggs's repertoire was modal in character, leaning heavily toward the minor. He recorded eight selections for Brunswick in 1927 and four more in 1929 for the extremely rare Lonesome Ace — Without a Yodel label.

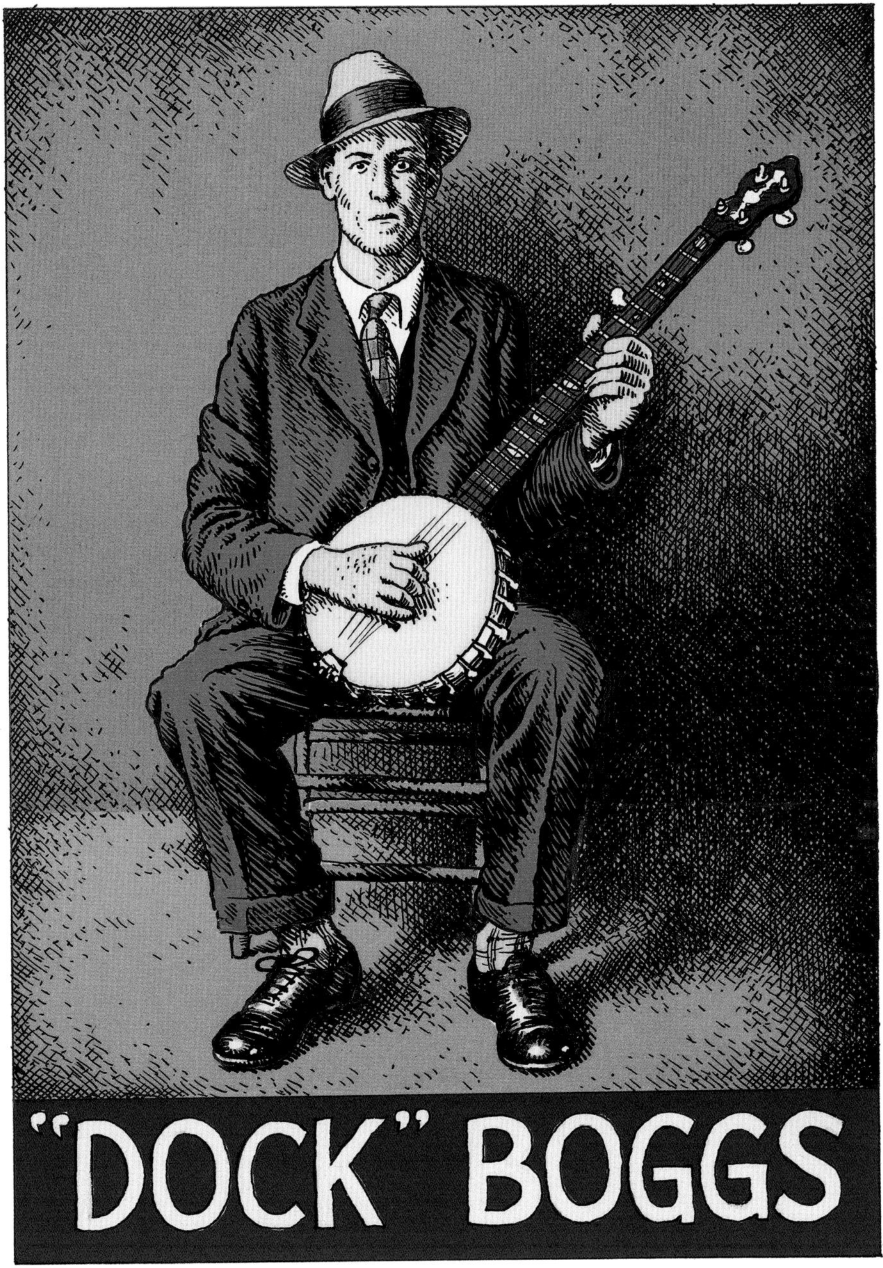
"DOCK" BOGGS

# FIDDLIN' POWERS & FAMILY

| Cowan Powers | Charlie Powers | Ada Powers | Opha Lou Powers | Carrie Belle Powers |
|---|---|---|---|---|
| FIDDLE | BANJO, VOCALS | UKULELE | MANDOLIN | GUITAR |
| B: *Russell County, Virginia* | B: *Russell County, Virginia* | B: *Russell County, Virginia* | B: *Russell County, Virginia* | B: *Russell County, Virginia* |
| D: *Unknown* | D: *Unknown* | D: *Unknown* | D: *Unknown* | D: *Unknown* |

No finer old-time traditional band ever recorded than Fiddlin' Powers & Family. The group was led by Cowan Powers, a masterful traditional musician who fiddled with broad, deep tone and commanding dynamics. His three daughters and son were the other members of the band. Charlie played banjo and sang, Ada played ukulele, Opha Lou played mandolin, and Carrie Belle played guitar.

The group's early acoustic (before the 1926 advent of electric microphones) recordings for Victor and Edison Records don't capture the real brilliance of their performances as do the four great electric selections made for Okeh Records in 1927, where Cowan's remarkable tone is especially apparent. Many old-time fiddlers were able to produce such full, rich, liquid tone, sounding almost as if their fiddles were filled with water. Today no one can reproduce the amazing tone of fiddlers like Powers, nor offer any explanation for how these old-timers did it. Adding greatly to the cohesive strength of the Powers band was the superb guitar playing of Carrie Belle. Byrd Moore had been an early tutor of hers and she herself shared ideas with the legendary Maybelle Carter, who lived near the Powers's Russell County, Virginia, home. Strangely enough for an instrument that is now viewed as a central component of most traditional American music, the guitar was scorned by most rural performers during its first few decades on the scene. It was stigmatized in its early days as a polite parlor instrument that was socially advantageous for young girls to play. It wasn't until the turn of the century that it began to become a significant instrument in both black and white music.

FIDDLIN' POWERS & FAMILY

# RED PATTERSON'S PIEDMONT LOG ROLLERS

**John Fletcher "Red" Patterson**
BANJO, VOCALS
B: *Near Leakesville, North Carolina, c. 1900*
D: *Unknown*

**Percy Setliff**
FIDDLE
B: *Unknown*
D: *Unknown*

**Dick Nolen**
BANJO
B: *Unknown*
D: *Unknown*

**Lee Nolen**
GUITAR
B: *Unknown*
D: *Unknown*

John Fletcher "Red" Patterson, born around 1900 near Leakesville, North Carolina, was a close friend and musical associate of Charlie Poole's and Kelly Harrell's. His band, the Piedmont Log Rollers, sounded very similar to both of theirs. The Log Rollers were especially smooth stylistically and their arrangements perfectly complemented the melancholy mood of most of the repertoire. Percy Setliff's sweet fiddling played the most important role in these arrangements, but Patterson's and Dick Nolen's banjos and Lee Nolen's guitar all worked together to produce a very tight-knit ensemble effect. Patterson's vocals were outstanding and the paramount factor of the group's fine performances. They recorded eight songs for Victor Records in 1927. The Log Rollers was a relatively informal group that played together mostly for dances and other social events sponsored by the clothing mills in the area.

**RED PATTERSON'S PIEDMONT LOG ROLLERS**

# WEEMS STRING BAND

| Dick Weems | Frank Weems | Jesse Weems | Alvin Conder |
|---|---|---|---|
| FIDDLE | FIDDLE | CELLO | BANJO, VOCALS |
| B: *Perry County, Tennessee* | B: *Perry County, Tennessee* | B: *Perry County, Tennessee* | B: *Perry County, Tennessee* |
| D: *Unknown* | D: *Unknown* | D: *Unknown* | D: *Unknown* |

Weems String Band recorded only one record, for Columbia Records in 1928, but this is considered by many to be the single finest white traditional recording of the period. The band's unusual style featured ultra-staccato phrasing and highly creative melodic variations usually led by the two fiddles playing in second and third position. It was highly unusual for rural fiddlers to play above first position. Second and third positions were almost always the domain of classically trained violinists. The Weems String Band, from deep in the backcountry of Perry County, Tennessee, would logically seem to be among the least likely candidates for using such sophisticated techniques. The doubly ironic observation is that the band produced, within the context of this sophisticated approach, the most primitive and archaic sound. This paradoxical contrast is at the heart of Weems's unique appeal. Brothers Dick and Frank were the fiddlers, and a third brother, Jesse, played bowed cello. Brother-in-law Alvin Conder played banjo and sang. Two younger family members not present on their records are shown far left and far right in the illustration (their names, unfortunately, are unknown). The band's use of variations of the basic melody put it in a league by itself. Few traditional groups had either the inclination or the imagination to use variations at all, and no group equaled the brilliant creativity of the Weems String Band.

WEEMS STRING BAND

# LEAKE COUNTY REVELERS

**Will (William Bryant) Gilmer**
FIDDLE
B: *Leake County, Mississippi, February 27, 1897*
D: *December 28, 1960*

**R. Oscar (R. O.) Moseley**
BANJO–MANDOLIN
B: *Sebastopol, Mississippi, 1885*
D: *c. 1930s*

**Jim Wolverton**
BANJO
B: *Leake County, Mississippi, April 1895*
D: *December 1969*

**Dallas Jones**
GUITAR, VOCALS
B: *Sebastopol, Mississippi, December 17, 1889*
D: *January 1985*

The style of the Leake County Revelers is perfectly representative of Mississippi's smooth-as-silk sound, due primarily to the brilliant, gliding fiddle playing of Will (William Bryant) Gilmer, whose technique is so liquid in tone it sounds as if there were oil on his strings. Constant slides in pitch facilitate Gilmer's exquisite tone, as does the usual Mississippi practice of tuning below standard pitch. The heart of this style lies in languid, finely con-toured bowing that opts for smoothly shaped notes rather than briskly animated tempo. Mississippi fiddlers usually streamlined the melody of fast dance tunes, eliminating many of the quick, syncopated figures of sixteenth and thirty-second notes that invigo-rated other southern versions with an insistent rhythmic pulse. They tended to play these tunes considerably slower than their counterparts in the southern mountains. The other Revelers band members were R. Oscar (R. O.) Moseley on banjo-mandolin, Jim Wolverton on banjo, and Dallas Jones on guitar and most lead vocals. The band recorded forty-four selections for Columbia Records, between 1927 and 1930, and was one of the best-selling groups of the period. The majority of the Revelers repertoire consisted of slow tunes with a loose, easy gait.

LEAKE COUNTY REVELERS

# WILMER WATTS OF WILMER WATTS AND THE LONELY EAGLES

**FIDDLE**

B: *Near Belmont, North Carolina, 1897*
D: *1943*

The music of Wilmer Watts is particularly interesting because it is so far removed geographically from the mainstream of white southern traditional music. Almost all white traditional performers documented on early records came from west of the eastern foothills of the Appalachian Mountains, where most of the music was to be found. White southern music is mostly Celtic in origin and was spread throughout the Appalachians by Scotch-Irish settlers who subsequently migrated predominantly in a western direction. Very few recordings were made documenting the music of the east-coast flatland South, where the purely English population remained dominant and played very little instrumental music. Watts came from near Belmont, North Carolina, a flatland area just forty miles from the Atlantic Ocean, and an area that had no other documentation at all. Watts and Wilson was the first of two Watts groups to record. The band featured—on its six 1927 Paramount Records selections—a totally unique steel guitar and banjo sound that worked so well it's surprising that nothing even similar was heard on any other recordings. The second Watts group, the Lonely Eagles, recorded fourteen songs for Paramount in 1929. These performances featured banjo and guitar played in a more mainstream fashion, especially the banjo, which opted for the more contemporary chording backup with little of the melody line style used in the first session. The vocals were outstanding, and featured perfect phrasing on both sessions. Watts worked for most of his life in textile mills. He was born in 1897 and died in 1943. His original records are among the most highly prized collector's items, not only for their rarity, but also for their distinctive brand of music and their unusual repertoire.

**WILMER WATTS**
of **WILMER WATTS** and
**THE LONELY EAGLES**

# SOUTH GEORGIA HIGHBALLERS

| **Melgie Ward** | **Vander Everidge** | **Albert Everidge** |
|---|---|---|
| FIDDLE | GUITAR | MUSICAL SAW |
| B: *Vicinity of Macon, Georgia* | B: *Vicinity of Macon, Georgia* | B: *Vicinity of Macon, Georgia* |
| D: *Unknown* | D: *Unknown* | D: *Unknown* |

The South Georgia Highballers were probably from around Macon. They recorded four selections for Okeh Records in 1927, featuring Melgie Ward on fiddle, Vander Everidge on guitar, and Albert Everidge on musical saw. The two title tracks, which feature guitar solos, are quite good. Although far from being one of the better bands, the Highballers had a very distinct style. The single most fascinating aspect of traditional American music is the endless variety of styles rural musicians could generate. Even within the context of strong regional traits, individual performers shaped their music with strikingly unique approaches. The considerable isolation of the early American countryside was a major factor in creating this bountiful panorama of styles. After hearing other players, most musicians were forced to re-create from memory by themselves in an isolated, rural environment. It is this transfer in this milieu that encourages the evolution of new musical styles. As evidence, trace the six or seven distinctly different fiddle styles brought to the United States from Northern Ireland and Scotland to the hundreds of American styles that evolved over the course of three or four generations. This heightened rate of change was aided in the States by the tendency to be musically self-taught, which contrasted with the more structured European system of studying with an older, skilled musician.

SOUTH GEORGIA
HIGHBALLERS

# HAPPY HAYSEEDS

| **Ivan Laam** | **Fred Laam** | **Bill Simmons** |
|---|---|---|
| FIDDLE | TENOR BANJO | GUITAR |
| B: *John Day, Oregon, c. 1900* | B: *John Day, Oregon, c. 1900* | B: *Unknown* |
| D: *Unknown* | D: *Unknown* | D: *Unknown* |

The Happy Hayseeds was one of the most fascinating bands of the period. Although the group's instrumentation of fiddle, tenor banjo, and guitar was common enough, its style was dramatically different from any other rural string band. Some of the Hayseeds' differences can be traced to their unique geographical and ethnic background. Ivan Laam, the fiddler, and his brother Fred, the banjo player, were born in John Day, Oregon, around 1900, whereas all other musicians from recorded string bands were from the South or Southwest. Most recorded rural white musicians' ancestors were early American settlers, but the Laam's were first-generation Americans. Their father, Abe Laam (a fiddler himself), migrated from Germany to Tennessee before moving to Oregon. The Laam family was in a totally different musical environment in Oregon from that which was documented on most rural recordings of the 1920s. They represent an intriguing byway of American music that has gone almost totally undocumented — a world of quadrilles, quicksteps, and other such quaint relics of old-time popular dancing. Judge Sturdy's Orchestra and Blind Uncle Gaspard recorded other delightful examples of this rare genre. Ivan's extensive use of vibrato and his frequent slurs in second position distinguish his excellent fiddling. Fred's banjo playing was technically brilliant, and absolutely charming for its whimsical embellishments. He played many and varied counter melodies with the fiddle, and frequently took the sole lead for many passages. The outstanding guitar was played by Bill Simmons, and provided an insistent tempo and deep, rich body for the music. The Laam family moved to California in the 1920s and it was there that the Hayseeds recorded their four issued selections for Victor Records.

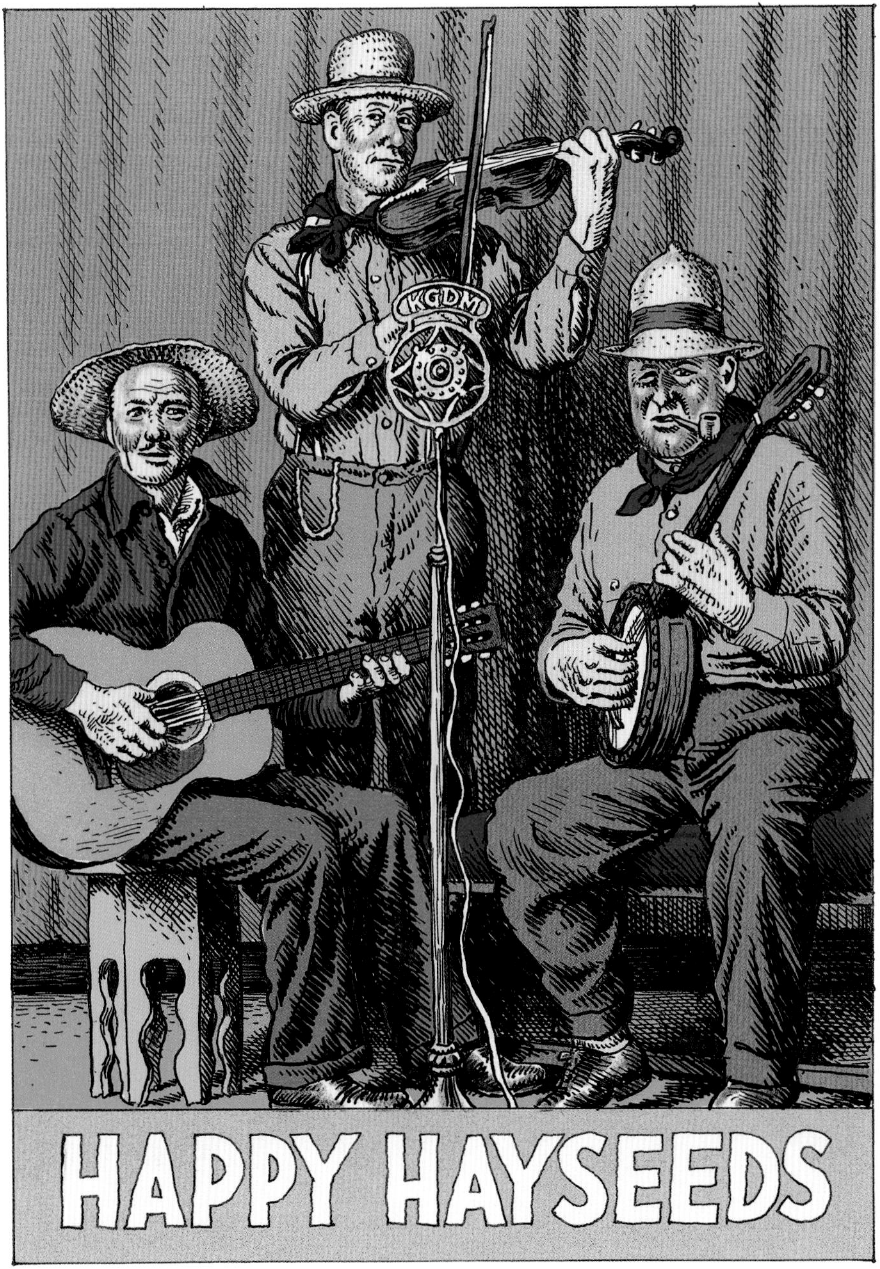
KGDM
HAPPY HAYSEEDS

# CROCKETT KENTUCKY MOUNTAINEERS

### John Harvey "Dad" Crockett
FIDDLE, BANJO
*B: Wayne County, West Virginia*
*D: Unknown*

### George Crockett
FIDDLE
*B: Bath County, Kentucky*
*D: Unknown*

### Johnny Crockett
BANJO, GUITAR, VOCALS
*B: Bath County, Kentucky*
*D: Unknown*

### Alan Crockett
FIDDLE, BONES
*B: Bath County, Kentucky*
*D: Unknown*

### Clarence Crockett
GUITAR
*B: Bath County, Kentucky*
*D: Unknown*

### Albert Crockett
TENOR GUITAR
*B: Bath County, Kentucky*
*D: Unknown*

Crockett's Kentucky Mountaineers was a superb country string band led by John Harvey "Dad" Crockett, who played fiddle and occasionally banjo. Crockett was born in Wayne County, West Virginia, and moved to Bath County, Kentucky, as a young man. The entire band was John and his children: George on fiddle; Johnny on banjo, guitar, and vocals; Alan on fiddle and bones; Clarence on guitar; and Albert on tenor guitar. As with all great family groups, the Crocketts played with consummate tightness. They had a thoroughly captivating gait, and easygoing syncopation. When their late 1920s recordings were made, they were living in their recently adopted California. They recorded first for Brunswick in Los Angeles and then for Crown Records in New York. Some of their Crown masters were also released on Paramount Records. Their Crown recording of "Little Rabbit/Rabbit Where's Your Mammy" is one of the finest rural string band performances.

CROCKETT KENTUCKY MOUNTAINEERS

# FOR NICK PERLS

**Acknowledgments:**

Special thanks to the following for their efforts in making this book possible:
Robert Crumb (without whom . . . ); Stephen Calt, David Jasen, and Richard Nevins
(for their incisive and informative text); Denis Kitchen and Judy Hansen (rights,
friendship, and the initial idea for this book); Charles Kochman and Eric Himmel
(editorial at Abrams); Miko McGinty and Rita Jules (for their inspired and respectful
design); Terry Zwigoff (introduction and insights); John Lind (for missing files and
supplementary material); and once again Richard Nevins at Yazoo Records/Shanachie
Entertainment (music, transparencies, and guidance).

**Editor:** Charles Kochman
**Designers:** Miko McGinty and Rita Jules
**Production Manager:** Kaija Markoe

Display type: Caslon's Egyptian
by Miko McGinty

**LIBRARY OF CONGRESS
CATALOGING-IN-PUBLICATION DATA**

Crumb, R.
　R. Crumb's heroes of blues, jazz & country /
illustrated by R. Crumb ; text by Stephen Calt,
David Jasen, and Richard Nevins ; introduction by Terry Zwigoff.
　　p. cm.
　ISBN 978-0-8109-3086-5 (hardcover
with jacket, includes 21-track audio cd)
　1. Blues musicians — Biography. 2. Jazz musicians — Biography. 3. Country musicians —
Biography. I. Crumb, R. II. Jasen, David A.
III. Nevins, Richard. IV. Title.

ML394.C35 2006
781.64092'273 — dc22

2006005835

*Heroes of the Blues* copyright © 1980, 1992, 1996,
2004 by Shanachie Entertainment Corp.
*Early Jazz Greats* copyright © 1982, 2005
Shanachie Entertainment Corp.
*Pioneers of Country Music* copyright © 1985, 2005
by Shanachie Entertainment Corp.
Compilation copyright © 2006 Denis Kitchen
Publishing Co. LLC

*Heroes of the Blues* text by Stephen Calt
*Early Jazz Greats* text by David Jasen
*Pioneers of Country Music* text by Richard Nevins

Printed and bound in China
10 9

Abrams books are available at special discounts
when purchased in quantity for premiums and
promotions as well as fundraising or educational
use. Special editions can also be created to spec-
ification. For details, contact specialmarkets@
hnabooks.com or the address below.

**HNA** ▮▮▮▮▮
**harry n. abrams, inc.**
a subsidiary of La Martinière Groupe
115 West 18th Street
New York, NY 10011
www.hnabooks.com

# BONUS MUSIC CD
# SELECTED AND COMPILED BY

# R. Crumb

## HEROES OF THE BLUES

1. **Memphis Jug Band** "On the Road Again"
2. **Blind Willie McTell** "Dark Night Blues"
3. **Cannon's Jug Stompers** "Minglewood Blues"
4. **Skip James** "Hard Time Killin' Floor Blues"
5. **Jaybird Coleman** "I'm Gonna Cross the River of Jordan —
Some O' These Days"
6. **Charley Patton** "High Water Everywhere"
7. **Frank Stokes** "I Got Mine"

## PIONEERS OF COUNTRY MUSIC

8. **"Dock" Boggs** "Sugar Baby"
9. **Shelor Family** "Big Bend Gal"
10. **Hayes Shepherd** "The Peddler and His Wife"
11. **Crockett's Kentucky Mountaineers** "Little Rabbit"
12. **Burnett & Rutherford** "All Night Long Blues"
13. **East Texas Serenaders** "Mineola Rag"
14. **Weems String Band** "Greenback Dollar"

## EARLY JAZZ GREATS

15. **Bennie Moten's Kansas City Orchestra** "Kater Street Rag"
16. **"King" Oliver's Creole Jazz Band** (w/ Louis Armstrong,
Johnny Dodds, Lil Hardin) "Sobbin' Blues"
17. **Parham-Pickett Apollo Syncopators**
(w/ "Tiny" Parham & Junie C. Cobb) "Mojo Strut"
18. **Frankie Franko & His Louisianians**
(w/ Ernest "Punch" Miller) "Somebody Stole My Gal"
19. **Clarence Williams' Blue Five** (w/ Sidney Bechet) "Wild Cat Blues"
20. **"Jelly Roll" Morton's Red Hot Peppers** "Kansas City Stomps"
21. **Jimmy Noone** "King Joe"

All of this music appears on various Yazoo Records CDs. These original recordings are
from 1927–31. To see and hear many more selections like these, visit *yazoorecords.com*